This belongs to....   April 8'

....David St Clair Shaw

Bought in London just down from Chancery
Lane, St Pauls(?) London, just before I met up
with Chris Groves and also before I also met
up with ✳Gus Ross, Neil Poulton, Maggie Latto,
Colin Burns, Alister Paul, John Innes (Chris
came with me!) Brilliant night — and so good
to see everyone.

Yours.
David StC Shaw
C. 86.

✳"HOG IN THE POUND" BOND ST.

PEOPLE-SPOTTING

AUTHORS' NOTES

SIMON BRETT is very Middle Class, a fact which causes him a considerable amount of Guilt. His Aspirations include writing crime novels, humorous books and scripts for radio and television; when they are not successful, he feels Disappointment. He lives with his wife and three children near Arundel, about which he feels appropriate Anxiety.

WENDY HUTTON is also Middle Class. She lives in East Sheen with her architect husband and two daughters, and does not feel that her Aspirations, Disappointments, Guilts and Anxieties are any of your business.

PEOPLE-SPOTTING
THE HUMAN SPECIES LAID BARE

BY SIMON BRETT
ILLUSTRATIONS WENDY HUTTON

ELM TREE BOOKS. LONDON

With Grateful Thanks to:

Christine Rowsell
Vicky Davey
John Godfrey
Norman Wild
Jill Davies
Henrietta Dennis
Dilys Zeegan
and
Fingal

First published in Great Britain 1985
by Elm Tree Books/Hamish Hamilton Ltd
Garden House 57-59 Long Acre London WC2E 9JZ

Book design by Wendy Hutton

British Library Cataloguing in Publication Data

Brett, Simon, 1945-
People-Spotting.
1. Human behavior–Anecdotes, facetiae,
satire, etc.
I. Title
150'.207 BF149.8

ISBN 0-241-11580-9

Typeset by Strobel & Sons,
11b Temple Sheen Rd., London SW14

Printed and bound in Great Britain by
R.J. Acford Ltd, Chichester

CONTENTS

DEDICATION-SPOTTING

It's never too soon to start PEOPLE-SPOTTING. So, instead of a wasted dedication page, as in most books, here is a short guide to the main types of dedications and what they say to the trained PEOPLE-SPOTTER about their authors:

TO MY MOTHER

(The author has probably failed to live up to her expectations in every other way, but at least now he's given her something solid she can show her friends.)

TO MY WIFE

(After the way he behaved to her while he was writing the thing, it's the very least he can do.)

TO MY CHILDREN,
WITHOUT WHOSE HELP THIS BOOK WOULD HAVE BEEN WRITTEN A LOT QUICKER

(You're in for something pretty dull here, gentle reader. Apart from the fact that he's trying to project himself as amazingly lovable, he also probably imagines he's the first person to have thought up that line.)

TO FIFI, WITH LOVE

(He's trying to perpetuate that old myth that writers are sexy, and imply that he has a lurid past. Unlikely to be true; most writers' lives are extraordinarily dull. Fifi's probably the cat.)

TO RODNEY,
WHO MADE ME WRITE IT

(This is a great cop-out. He's trying to absolve himself from responsibility. If everyone thinks it's a load of cobblers, he wants them to blame Rodney.)

TO GEORGE,
WHO TAUGHT ME ALL I KNOW

(Same as above. Why should poor old George carry the can?)

TO MR. WALLACE,
MY FIRST ENGLISH MASTER, WHO AWAKENED MY INTEREST IN LITERATURE

(Now he's just being patronising. Also he's trying to imply that his book should be classified as "literature" - cheeky bugger!)

TO THE ISLE OF ARRAN

(He's doing the old Wordsworthian bit, projecting himself as the writer with the private hotline to nature.)

TO MOLLY, FRED, WIMBO, TURKEY, BAZ, NEBULA AND ALL AT THE GAZEBO

(He's just showing off about what a wild social life he leads. Probably not true.)

TO MARGARET THATCHER, THE FINEST LADY IN THE LAND

(The lengths some people will go to to get an O.B.E...)

INTRODUCTION

People's every action reveals something about themselves. What they do, where they do it, what they say, how they say it, what they own and why they bought it all give clues to a person's nature. But since most people spend a large part of their time obscuring what they're really up to, understanding the true meaning of their behaviour can sometimes prove tricky.

The aim of this book is to train its readers to recognise the real meaning of the various statements which are given out, to see through the layers of deceit and pretension with which people surround themselves. This process is known as PEOPLE-SPOTTING, and those who follow the book assiduously will become expert PEOPLE-SPOTTERS.

Like all works of pseudoscience, this one is full of sweeping statements, rash generalisations and incomplete arguments, because research (inadequate research, of course) has revealed that this is what the public has come to expect of this kind of book. It is also full of jargon, categories, charts and lists, so that the reader can attain that level of self-congratulatory elitism to which such books aspire.

Most important of all, in common with others of the genre, PEOPLE-SPOTTING describes people in such a way that, though readers can tut pityingly at the foibles of others, they will never have to identify themselves to their disadvantage.

1. INTENTIONS AND REACTIONS

Everything people do has two values. There is the INTENTION (how they think people are going to react to what they do), and the REACTION (how people actually react to what they do). These two values rarely coincide.

The INTENTION is always to give someone else a message that will elicit a specific response. The commonest messages that people try to give out are the following:

A. I am successful.
B. I am efficient.
C. I am sexy.
D. I am charmingly vulnerable
E. I am honest.
F. I am clever.
G. I am discriminating.
H. There is more to me than meets the eye.

All of these messages are meant to elicit the same response, which is:

Admire me.

However, that response is only rarely achieved. Much more common REACTIONS are:

1. I don't trust you.
2. I don't like you.
3. I disagree.
4. What an idiot.

In other words, people, knowing their own deviousness, are very wary of taking anything anyone else offers them at face value.
In the course of this book, PEOPLE-SPOTTERS will quickly find themselves able to recognise the relevant INTENTIONS and REACTIONS in a variety of situations.

2. CLASS

Much has been written about the British class system, and the tendency of most authorities has been to overcomplicate the issue. PEOPLE-SPOTTERS may rest assured that the subject is in fact very simple.

There are only four classes in this country and they are the following:

ARISTOCRATS, THE RICH, WORKING CLASS and MIDDLE CLASS.

As a PEOPLE-SPOTTER, you can discover the class of anyone you meet by the following method. You have simply to ask the question:

"What class are you?",

and analyse the reply given according to the notes overleaf.

1. People who do not understand the question are automatically ARISTOCRATS. They don't understand it because, having taken everything for granted from birth, it is not a subject they've ever had to think about.
(There are very few ARISTOCRATS about, so PEOPLE-SPOTTERS need not worry about them.)

2. THE RICH may answer the question in a variety of ways, but they are certain to let you know within thirty seconds that they've got a lot of money. Incidentally, people who apologise for the fact that they've got a lot of money are not authentic members of THE RICH; they are, by definition, MIDDLE CLASS.
(There are more of THE RICH than there are ARISTOCRATS, but still not that many, so PEOPLE-SPOTTERS do not have to bother with them either.)

3. The WORKING CLASS will reply to your question without hesitation, "Working Class," frequently adding, "…and proud of it". Though the title is all too often an inaccurate description in modern Britain, those who belong to this class have no doubts about their social status.
N.B. You should be warned not to believe this reply when it is uttered by an actor, writer, M.P. or Trade Union leader, all of whom, whatever their origins may have been, have by definition joined the MIDDLE CLASS.
(There are, by the way, very few authentic members of the WORKING CLASS, so they, too, need not concern PEOPLE-SPOTTERS.)

4. Anyone who hesitates in replying to your question is automatically MIDDLE CLASS. So is anyone who claims not to know which class they belong to, or who qualifies their reply with comparative adjectives like *"Upper"* or *"Lower"*. Members of the MIDDLE CLASS lack the security and stability of the other three classes. They never are anywhere socially; they've either just come from somewhere or are just going somewhere; they are either on the way up or on the way down. The identifying marks of the MIDDLE CLASS are GUILT and ANXIETY, ASPIRATION and DISAPPOINTMENT. (The vast majority of people in this country are MIDDLE CLASS.)
As a result, this book deals almost exclusively with the MIDDLE CLASS, and the PEOPLE-SPOTTER's viewpoint, in discussion of human behaviour, is the exact middle of the MIDDLE CLASS. There are many reasons for this, but the main one is that the MIDDLE CLASS are the people who buy books.

3. NAMES

When two people are introduced, their first feeling is one of mutual distrust. The level of that distrust is controlled by many factors — by the people's physical qualities, by their clothes, by how they speak, by where the meeting takes place, by background information previously supplied by (usually malicious) third parties, etc.

The level of distrust is also affected by the NAMES of the people introduced. Each individual has his own scale of suspicion for various names, because everyone has different grounds for prejudice. Some hate the name NIGEL because it was the name of a boy who used to beat them up in the school playground. Some can't stand SHIRLEY because it brings back an unfortunate memory of unrequited teenage love. Some are appalled to be introduced to a person called MAX because it makes them think of a television celebrity they particularly dislike. And so on, and so on.

But the Middle Class is an easy class to generalise about (particularly in a book like this), and so certain general rules can be (or at least are going to be) extrapolated. It is important that PEOPLE-SPOTTERS should be able to recognise the degrees of distrust generated by various names in the prejudiced Middle Class mind (and all Middle Class minds are, by definition, prejudiced).
Overleaf are Easy-to-Follow, At-A-Glance charts for Men's Names and Women's Names, which will make everything clear.

MEN'S NAMES:

Andrew	Andy	Adam	Cedric
Charles	Charlie	Adrian	Dudley
Christopher	Chris	Alan	Edmund
David	Dave	Anthony	Frederick
John	Johnnie	Benjamin	George
Martin	Marty	Bernard	Giles
Michael	Mike	Daniel	Godfrey
Peter	Pete	Dennis	Henry
Richard	Dick	Edward	James
		Geoffrey	Jeremy
YOU MAY BE ALL RIGHT.	THAT MATINESS DOESN'T FOOL ME	Graham	Matthew
		Hugh	Miles
		Jonathan	Oliver
		Mark	Roland
		Nicholas	Sebastian
		Nigel	William
		Paul	
		Philip	I BET YOU'RE NOT REALLY UPPER CLASS.
		Robert	
		Roger	
		Thomas	
		Timothy	
		Simon	

I DON'T TRUST YOU, BUT I'M NOT QUITE SURE WHY YET. GIVE ME TIME.

Albert
Alfred
Arthur
Barry
Brian
Bruce
Clive
Colin
Daryl
Derek
Eric
Gary
Harold
Herbert
Joseph
Keith
Kenneth
Kevin
Lester
Marvin
Maurice
Neville
Norman
Raymond
Reginald
Ronald
Roy
Sidney
Stanley
Terence

I THINK YOU'RE BENEATH ME SOCIALLY, WHICH MAKES ME FEEL SUPERIOR (BUT I STILL DON'T TRUST YOU).

Alastair
Angus
Brendan
Connor
Dermot
Douglas
Duncan
Gareth
Griffith
Hamish
Patrick
Rory
Stuart

YOU'RE VIRTUALLY FOREIGN.

Ambrose
Aubrey
Barnaby
Crispin
Hilary
Hugo
Jason
Jocelyn
Julian
Melvyn
Tristram

I AM EXTREMELY SUSPICIOUS OF YOU. YOU MIGHT EVEN BE GAY.

Archibald
Basil
Benedict
Clarence
Claud
Clement
Hector
Horace
Osbert
Oswald
Peregrine
Rollo
Sylvester
Vivian

THAT'S A BLOODY SILLY NAME.

WOMEN'S NAMES

Ann	Annie	Barbara	Alexandra
Elizabeth	Liz	Carol	Amanda
Catherine	Kate	Caroline	Arabella
Jane	Janie	Clare	Camilla
Susan	Sue	Diana	Candida
		Elaine	Drusilla
YOU MAY BE ALL	**THAT MATINESS**	Gillian	Felicity
RIGHT. I'LL WAIT	**DOESN'T FOOL ME**	Heather	Lucinda
AND SEE.		Helen	Melissa
		Isabel	Miranda
		Jacqueline	Roberta
		Janet	
		Jennifer	**I BET YOU'RE NOT**
		Jill	**REALLY UPPER**
		Judith	**CLASS.**
		Juliet	
		Margaret	
		Marian	
		Mary	
		Pamela	
		Patricia	
		Penelope	
		Rosemary	
		Sarah	
		Sally	
		Vivien	

**I DON'T TRUST YOU,
BUT I'M NOT QUITE
SURE WHY YET.
GIVE ME TIME.**

Angela   Marie
Anthea   Marilyn
Audrey   Maureen
Avril   Norma
Beryl   Pauline
Brenda   Rita
Cynthia   Ruby
Daphne   Sandra
Dawn   Sheila
Deirdre   Shirley
Denise   Silvia
Doris   Stella
Doreen   Theresa
Dorothy   Thelma
Edna   Valerie
Fay   Vera
Gay   Violet
Gladys
Gloria
Hilda
Ida
Iris
Ivy
Joyce
June
Kim
Linda
Lorna
Lorraine

Ailsa
Bernadette
Blodwyn
Bridget
Bronwen
Catriona
Flora
Siobhan

**YOU'RE VIRTUALLY
FOREIGN.**

Abigail   Adelaide
Alice   Amaryllis
Antonia   Charmian
Beatrice   Christabel
Charlotte   Eunice
Claudia   Hermoine
Cressida   Imogen
Eleanor   Jemima
Frances   Lalage
Hannah   Perpetua
Harriet   Phoebe
Hilary   Tabitha
Jessica
Laura   **THAT'S A BLOODY
Olivia   SILLY NAME.**
Rebecca
Ursula
Victoria
Virginia

**I AM EXTREMELY
SUSPICIOUS OF YOU.
YOU MIGHT EVEN BE
AN INTELLECTUAL.**

**I THINK YOU'RE
BENEATH ME
SOCIALLY, WHICH
MAKES ME FEEL
SUPERIOR (BUT I
STILL DON'T TRUST
YOU).**

SURNAMES

Surnames, too, provoke distrust, but there are so many of them that it is difficult to give more than general rules on the subject. However, the following guidelines will prove of use to PEOPLE-SPOTTERS in gauging degrees of distrust:

1. Obviously regional surnames (e.g. McTavish, O'Brien, ap Griffith) or obviously ethnic surnames (e.g. Goldstein, Malinowski, Patel) prompt extremely juvenile initial reactions, which can best be discovered by reading any book of old jokes.

2. Surnames which also exist as words of mildly humorous meaning (e.g. Grubb, Mudd, Virgo) prompt reactions in adults which would seem unsophisticated in a primary school playground. Owners of such names get inured to the sniggers they cause, and have to keep reminding themselves that for someone who hasn't heard it before even the oldest joke still contains some element of humour.

3. Peculiar surnames which are claimed to be Huguenot in origin brand their owners not only to be foreign, but also pretentious.

4. Surnames which are pronounced differently from the way they are spelt (e.g. Cholmondley, Dalziel, Featherstone) make the Middle Class extremely suspicious. Initially, they refuse to believe that the name is genuine; and once they have been convinced of that, they become terrified that the owner of the name is about to borrow money from them.

5. Surnames which do not begin with capitals (french, etc.) throw the Middle Class into paroxysms of suspicion.

6. Hyphenated surnames make them even more suspicious.

7. Hyphenated surnames of which the second part is "Smith" or "Jones" are always greeted with glee by members of the Middle Class. At last, they feel confident, they have met someone even more socially insecure than they are themselves.

APPEARANCE 4

From primitive times onwards people have always been trying to change what they look like. Whether their medium of disguise is woad or Max Factor, tatooing or cosmetic surgery, the urge to look different remains strong. It doesn't take a very sophisticated knowledge of psychology to deduce that this instinct arises from people's basic insecurity, their fear of facing the world as themselves in an unadorned state.

Needless to say, the Middle Class, who have raised insecurity almost to an art-form, are particularly keen on disguise and camouflage. It is instinctive for them to try and present themselves as other than what they really are. Like very confused birds being filmed by David Attenborough, they spend much of their time giving out Appearance Signals designed to mislead observers. Trained PEOPLE-SPOTTERS, however, never allow themselves be deceived by such displays.

The main methods of camouflage used by the Middle Class concentrate either on just the head, or on all the rest of the body. Since the face is by far the most expressive part of the human animal, much effort is spent in hiding its expressiveness with such devices as hair-style, make-up, facial hair and glasses. (Examples of the use of some of these are given later in this section.)

The rest of the body is camouflaged with clothes. Even when a representative of the Middle Class is stripped to the minimum (i.e. topless on a beach in Corfu), the nature of the remaining wisp of cloth still makes a statement about its wearer. And the more clothes that are piled on to the Middle Class frame, the more misleading Appearance Signals are given off.
Basically, people dress to gain time, to steal a march on others whom they meet. If they can give an initial impression which is misleadingly favourable, they have gained a small advantage, on which they can enlarge even when their true identity becomes known.
In the following pages, PEOPLE-SPOTTERS will be trained to recognise some of the more common Middle Class misleading Appearance Signals.

WOMEN'S CLOTHES

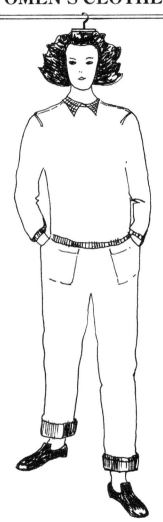

Highly complex, university-educated housewife and mother asserting her essential simplicity.

Housewife and mother on shopping trip to London, trying to pass herself off as somebody who actually works there.

Housewife who has recently given up working due to husband's promotion, dressed for coffee morning.

Housewife who mistakenly believes that there is such a thing as classic style in dress.

Housewife and mother who believes everything she reads in in Shirley Conran and *Cosmopolitan.*

Acquisitive, unimaginative housewife trying to pass herself off as unmaterialistic and/or artistic.

MEN'S CLOTHES

Suburban man dressed for Saturday morning shopping at Waitrose.

Actor or writer who slopes around in pullovers all day, dressed for dinner party.

Businessman who wears suit all day, dressed for dinner party.

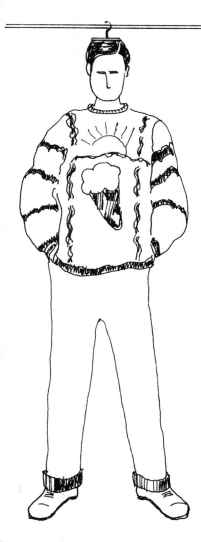

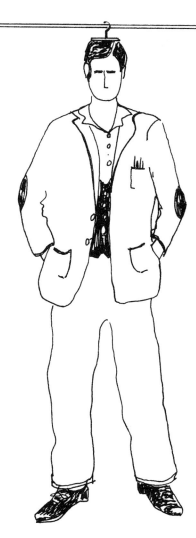

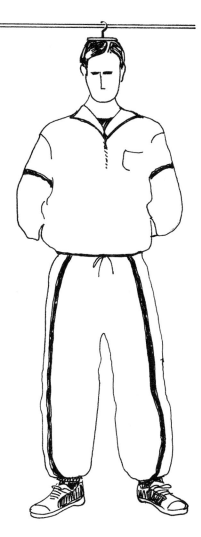

Unscrupulous television or advertising executive camouflaged as Playschool presenter.

Man who believes that shabby traditional dress makes him melt into his surroundings (unaware that he sticks out like a sore thumb).

Suburban man dressed for Sunday morning car washing.

INDIVIDUAL GARMENTS

It would be impossible to list all of the garments which give rise to major discrepancies between the wearer's INTENTION and the spectator's REACTION, but the following list covers some of them. (The sex of the wearer of the garment is indicated by the letter "M" or "F".)

GARMENT	INTENTION	REACTION
ARAN SWEATER (M or F)	(M) "I look rugged." (F) "I look sporty, but a bit waiflike."	"I bet that tickles."
BELT, THICK WITH LARGE BUCKLE (M)	"Pretty macho, huh?"	"What a large paunch."
BOW TIE (M)	"Don't I look smart and interesting?"	"I wonder what he's compensating for?"
COWBOY BOOTS (M)	"I look tough."	"You're trying to look taller, aren't you?"
DEERSTALKER (M)	"Anyone can see that I am wearing this as a rather sophisticated joke."	"What an absolute pratt!"
DENIM CAP (M)	"I am unmaterialistic."	"Pity about John Lennon, wasn't it?"
DIAMOND-PATTERNED PULLOVER (M)	"I look really relaxed."	"Ugh! He looks like Val Doonican."
DR. SCHOLL'S WOODEN CLOGS (F)	"These make me look really practical."	"Don't those sandals make women's calves look a funny shape?"
DUFFEL COAT (M)	"I look solid and reliable."	"He looks like Paddington Bear."
DUNGAREES (F)	"I look practical without losing my my essential femininity."	"You look like a sack of potatoes."
GUERNSEY SWEATER (M or F)	"I look as if I have roots."	"Another *Observer* Special Offer, I see."
KILT (M or F)	(M) "I am proud of my Scottish ancestry." (F) "I am sensible."	"Oh, God, he's going to start talking about his Scottish ancestry." "I wonder what committee she's on."

GARMENT	INTENTION	REACTION
LEATHER TROUSERS (M or F)	(M) "These really make me feel like a stud." (F) "These make me look really sexy."	(M or F) "It must be jolly sweaty in those."
MINK COAT (F)	"This really shows them I'm someone."	"I wonder what she had to do to get that…?"
POP-SOCKS (F)	"These look just as if I've got tights on."	"She hasn't got tights on – I can see a bit of bare knee."
REAL SILK DRESS (F)	"Anyone can see this is real silk."	"That's never real silk."
SHEEPSKIN COAT (M)	"I've made it."	"Oh God, a second-hand car salesman!"
SMOCK (F)	"I look charmingly unaffected."	"She must have a terrible figure."
TIGHTS WITH PATTERNS ON THEM (F)	"These show off my legs to full advantage."	"She looks as if she's got some skin disease."
TONING SHIRT AND TIE SET (M)	"I look like an executive."	"Oh God, a salesman!"

FACIAL HAIR

Man is the only animal species which shaves. Many explanations have been put forward for this fact, but the most likely seems to be that he is also the only animal species which can use a razor. Though in the natural state, his facial hair would be allowed to grow freely, man has now been shaving for so long that the smooth face has become the norm, and beards and moustaches are the exception. So, like all exceptions or divergences from the norm, they are used to make statements.

The main statement made by any beard or moustache is
"I AM COMPENSATING FOR SOMETHING."

Like heavy make-up on a woman, a beard or moustache on a man expresses an unwillingness to face the world unadorned — at its most basic, a feeling that there is something wrong with him. Needless to say, different kinds of facial hair make different individual statements (and of course get different reactions).

MOUSTACHES:

THE "INGROWING TOENAIL"

Once popular in the R.A.F., surely no one can still use that as an excuse for growing this one. It may signify that the wearer chairs Victorian Music Hall Evenings for his local Amateur Operatic Society, but otherwise its appearance is one of nature's unexplained mysteries.
REACTION : "Why on earth would anyone want to go around looking like that?"

THE "ITALIAN WAITER"

This is probably the most basic form of moustache. For anyone whose hair is dark, its effect is to make them look exactly like an Italian waiter.
REACTION : "He looks exactly like an Italian waiter."

THE "WHAT'S THAT FUNNY LITTLE LINE ACROSS HIS UPPER LIP?"

This is the one that was favoured by Forties movie stars and certain sorts of insecure military men. Its other name, the "pencil" moustache, probably arises from the fact that it looks as if someone's been scribbling on the wearer's face.
REACTION : "Surely shaving round that every morning's more trouble than it's worth."

THE "WOFFLY"

This one has the effect (and is intended to have the effect) of making the wearer look a bit bumbling and ineffectual. It is often complemented by spectacles.
REACTION : "How on earth does he manage when he eats corn-on-the-cob?"

THE "SAD FACE"

This one is affected by people (usually in very safe jobs with good pensions) who like to be thought of as radical.
REACTION: "Is he a relic of the Sixties growing a Zapata or is he a trendy leftie growing a Lech Walesa?"

BEARS:

THE "ALEXANDER SOLZHENITSYN"

This one might look better if the wearer's head was the other way up.
REACTION: "I bet his moustache doesn't grow properly."

THE "GRANDEE"

This is the neat little beard-and-moustache set favoured by Spanish grandees in paintings by El Greco. On his elongated figures it could look quite good. Unfortunately nowadays it's usually worn by short, chubby men and has the effect of making them look shorter and chubbier
REACTION : "He can't really think that makes him look distinguished. Can he?"

THE "HOBBIT"

This is the beard of someone who has curly hair and never shaves. It generates a comfortingly fuzzy outline and its wearers tend also to wear fuzzy pullovers. It is a look much favoured by short, round engineers who don't change their pullovers as regularly as one might wish.
REACTION : "Actually, he probably wouldn't look that much better without a beard."

THE "FALSE BEARD"

The kind favoured by Victorian patriarchs, this one moves rigidly when the head is moved and gives the impression that it is held on to the ears by curved wires.
REACTION : "Well, I suppose it saves having to wear a tie."

THE "TOPIARIST"

The wearer of this sort of beard and moustache regards his face as an artistic medium, and actually *sculpts* his facial hair. He keeps the growth very short and if there is any bit he can shave round or between, he shaves round or between it. This obsessive neatness is usually reflected in an infuriatingly nitpicking personality.
REACTION : "God, it must take him hours to do that every morning."

THE "ARAFAT"

Much favoured by media people, this hardly qualifies as a beard, being no more than three days' growth of stubble. Its intention is to make the wearer look as if he's just got out of bed after a three-day orgy. What is remarkable is how it is kept at that length. Though he never lets it grow into a proper beard, the wearer is never seen clean-shaven. This makes it another of nature's unexplained mysteries.
REACTION : "Oh yes, very macho, I don't think."

GLASSES

People used not to have any control over their glasses; they just had to wear what was available. But the introduction of contact lenses and the wide variety of frame styles now available means that almost everyone wears glasses which they think *DO SOMETHING FOR THEM.* As ever, the wearer's INTENTION is frequently at odds with the observer's REACTION, as demonstrated in the following illustrations:

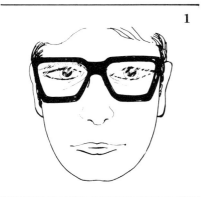

1

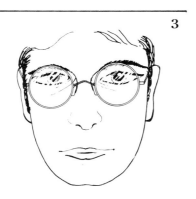

3

1 THICK-FRAMED CONVENTIONAL GLASSES
INTENTION : "These make me look efficient and incisive."
REACTION : "If you took the glasses away you wouldn't notice him."

2 RECTANGULAR GLASSES SHAPED LIKE TELEVISION SCREENS
INTENTION : "These give my face character."
REACTION : "He looks totally characterless."

3 LITTLE ROUND WIRE-FRAMED GLASSES
INTENTION : "By wearing these, I am sending up the concept of glasses. By going for the most basic, old-fashioned style, I am asserting my independence of materialism. These glasses show me to be a complex and interesting character."
REACTION : "He looks just like a Nazi doctor from a 'B'-movie."

4 WIRE-FRAMED HALF-GLASSES
INTENTION : "These make me look mature, reliable, avuncular…spiritual even."
REACTION : "He looks as if he's strayed out of a BBC2 Classic Serial."

2

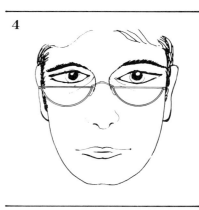

4

5

6

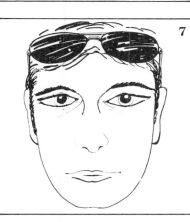

7

8

5   BRIGHTLY-COLOURED LARGE-FRAME UPSIDE DOWN GLASSES

INTENTION : "These show I've got a bit of dash. The coloured frames make an interesting counterpoint to my conventional suit, indicating that there is more to me than meets the eye, that in fact I'm a bit of a gay dog."

REACTION : "He looks as if he's got his glasses on upside down."

6   MOTOR-RACING-TYPE DARK GLASSES WITH REFLECTING FRONTS

INTENTION : "These make me look enigmatic…intriguing…a bit sexy…"

REACTION : "What a creep."

7   ROUND SUNGLASSES WORN ON THE FOREHEAD

INTENTION : "I look like a very laid-back member of the international jet set."

REACTION : "I wonder if he realises he's got those things on his forehead…"

8   MONOCLE

INTENTION : "Of course, as I always tell people (at great length) I wear a monocle because I only have impaired vision in one eye and this is the most practical form of lens for that deficiency. However, I am also aware that it makes me look a charmingly eccentric person, distinguished, artistic …striking."

REACTION : "What a twit!"

One of the most obvious uses of facial hair and glasses is to disguise the age of the wearer. Baby-faced adolescents often grow beards, and so do young men suddenly promoted to levels they feel to be above their years.

For similar reasons, habitual beard-wearers approaching the Male Menopause frequently shave off their growths. (This is particularly true of those whose beards grow grey before the rest of their hair . Forty-year-olds are frequently to be observed shaving their sideburns higher and higher as the tell-tale white hairs advance up their cheeks.)

Glasses can be used in the same way. The secretary who finally attains an executive position often dons heavy-rimmed spectacles to make her look more mature and formidable.

But both devices remain primarily means of camouflage, to be used (like bow-ties) by those who don't believe that their identities will register without such props. Of course, the person who uses all three disguises (facial hair, glasses and bow-tie) really has got problems.

HABITAT

Apart from what they look like, for most people where they live is the biggest opportunity they get to make a statement about themselves. Though very few actually build houses to their own designs, the changes that they make to the ones they do live in are extremely informative for the keen PEOPLE-SPOTTER.

Middle Class people impose their personalities on their homes in three main ways. The first is apparently low-profile, the other two more assertive (though all three require a great deal of calculations and effort). The statements made by the three approaches are, respectively:

1. We have been here for ever.
2. We've really made some improvements.
3. We are people of exceptional taste.

And, though one might think that the evidence of such approaches would be slow to manifest itself, it is in fact clear from the day that the owners of the house move in.

Those favouring the first approach aim to recreate their home as it was when originally built. Frequently extremely acquisitive upwardly mobile couples, they try to make their houses look unaffectedly simple, with much evidence of Laura Ashley, stripped pine, mud-coloured paint, old photographs and agricultural implements on the walls. The effect is usually like something out of *Upstairs Downstairs.*

The second approach tries to deny the history of the house. It is based on the belief that the original structure can be totally concealed by a sufficient number of patio doors and sealed aluminium-framed double-glazed window units. Indeed, this is the home of the unit. The kitchen is full of units, the main reception room has a room-dividing unit, and the bathrooms of course contain vanitory units.

The third is the province of people who work in design (architects, television designers, etc.) or, more fatally, unqualified people who believe they have a *flair* for the subject. For them their home is just another medium in which to express their artistic abilities.

These attitudes affect the whole living environment, the house's exterior, interior and garden – as can be seen from the ensuing illustrations.

EXTERIORS

1   "It makes us feel part of the history of the area…"

2   "Of course we wanted to get one of those new houses up on the estate, but…"

3   "Oh, you can't miss our house – we've really *thought* about what it looks like…"

INTERIORS

1 "No, not consciously
collected – they're just bits
and pieces we like...
have some more quiche..."

2　"Perhaps you'd like to come through from the drinks area to the audio area... how about some James Last...?"

3　"This is our living space... where we, you know, live... in the fullest sense..."

GARDENS

1 "And, quite honestly, except for the aeroplane noise, you could imagine you're in the middle of the country..."

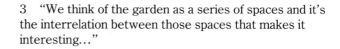

2   "Why don't we drink our Sangria on the patio...?"

3   "We think of the garden as a series of spaces and it's the interrelation between those spaces that makes it interesting..."

THE LONDON AREA LYING GAME

People have always lied about where they live. Encouraged by the roseate prose of estate agents, they have always tended to home in on the adjacent area which best fits in with their aspirations. This is particularly true in London, where greater anonymity and population density makes such lies less likely to be identified. (The giveaway for the acute PEOPLE-SPOTTER is any hesitation or qualification of the area in response to the question, "Where do you live?")

The following chart makes clear what people really mean. On the left is the statement of location made in response to the query at a middle-class dinner party, and on the right is its true meaning:

WE LIVE	TRUE LOCATION
Barnesish	East Sheen
in good old Bayswater	Paddington
pretty well Blackheath	Lewisham
on the edge of Chelsea	Pimlico
not far from Cheyne Walk	Battersea
well, I suppose it's Dulwich, really	Herne Hill
round Ealing	Acton
down near Greenwich	Charlton
sort of Hampstead	Kilburn
in trendy Hackney	Leyton
not a million miles from Holland Park	Shepherd's Bush
Islington fringes	Stoke Newington
kind of Kensington	Olympia
within walking distance of Kew Gardens	Brentford
down Richmond way	Isleworth

(N.B. One should also be on the look-out for inverted snobbery. Very few left-wing white schoolteachers who say they live in Brixton actually do.)

6. POSSESSIONS

Once the PEOPLE-SPOTTER'S subject of study, the member of the Middle Class, has organised its appearance and habitat to be suitably misleading, its attention is focused on the accessories with which it surrounds itself. The aim of all possessions, like everything else in Middle Class life, is to emit messages about their owner.

Despite constant protestations of poverty, and constant assertions of how little material things matter, the modern Middle Class is one of the most acquisitive sectors of society which has ever existed. Its materialism should be measured not so much by what it buys, but by the state of repair of what it throws away. Local council refuse tips provide the most telling evidence. Difficulties in getting anything repaired (despite the enormous growth of the service sector of the work-force) and sheer laziness have combined to encourage the **"It doesn't work, let's get another one"** philosophy. From that attitude it is only a small step to **"It looks old-fashioned, let's get another one."**

As ever, **Middle Class Anxiety About What Other People Might Think** dominates their motivation. While it may look strikingly original to have a Thirties "sunburst" radio or a wind-up gramophone with a horn, a five-year-old Japanese music centre can look just tacky. The owners are too insecure to wait until Japanese music centres become collectors' items, so out they go to be replaced by the latest models (usually the same components reorganised behind a different facade).

The same **Anxiety** urges them to invest in the newest technology. Home computers provide a perfect example of the Middle Class rush not to be outdone by their neighbours. In 1984 in particular, any number of specious excuses (organising household accounts, filing recipes, printing out Christmas card lists, etc.) were produced by adults to justify the initial investment. After the first week the computer was used only for games; after the second week it was used for games only by the children; and after the third month in most cases it was relegated to the shelf.

In the ensuing pages, Middle Class attitudes to possessions are spelled out more fully, with particular reference to **Cars, Books, Magazines and Pets.**

CARS

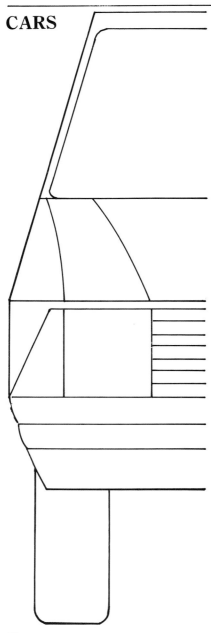

THE "YOU KNOW WHAT IT'S LIKE WHEN YOU'VE GOT CHILDREN" CAR

Owners of these are the sort of people who feel that having had children exonerates them from all other responsibilities in life. The car is probably a large hatchback up to five years old. The big Peugeot with three rows of seats is ideal.
Of course it has child seats, and there is always plenty of other evidence of juvenile occupation – broken plastic toys, buggies, pencils, sweet packets, half-eaten buns, paintings from playschool, spaceships made out of egg-boxes, etc. Anyone unwise enough to reach into the crevices of the back seats in such vehicles will encounter a noxious compound of crushed crisps, biscuit crumbs, damp toffee, sand and, probably, congealed vomit.
STATEMENT : *"AREN'T WE LOVABLE?"*

THE "PLUTOCRAT" CAR

A Rolls-Royce, Porsche, Lamborghini, etc.
STATEMENT : *"I'M JOLLY RICH - SO THERE!"*

THE "CONNOISSEUR" CAR

This is a car of obscure but reputable make (ideally one that has gone out of business like a Riley). It is the owner's pride and joy, and no conversational *non sequitur* is too remote to prompt a monologue about the car's technical details.
PEOPLE-SPOTTERS are urgently advised to avoid such owners at all costs.
STATEMENT :*"I AM A PERSON OF REMARKABLE DISCRIMINATION."*

THE "COME ON, PRUDENCE, YOU CAN MAKE IT" CAR

This is the Car-as-Pet, much favoured by single girls in their twenties and thirties. It is talked to constantly as it is coaxed and cajoled up hills. Potential boyfriends should always be able to get the car going when it finally grinds to a halt, but should never commit the heresy of suggesting that the owner gets something more practical.
STATEMENT : *"AREN'T I DELICIOUSLY SCATTER-BRAINED?"*

THE "BIT OF POWER UNDER THE BONNET" CAR

This tends to be something like an Alfa Sud or BMW, and is favoured by people in Marketing (i.e. salesmen) who don't have to have a Ford. Such owners subscribe to the outdated theory that powerful cars bestow an image of sexual potency on their drivers.
STATEMENT : *"I AM QUITE A STUD."*

THE "FACTORY-FRESH" CAR

This has been owned from new by a gentlemen who is now retired. Many are to be seen on the roads of the South Coast, driven doggedly at 35 m.p.h. Their bodywork sparkles, their chrome and windows gleam. The seats probably have covers. The steering wheel certainly does, and the driver wears string-backed

leather driving gloves.
STATEMENT : *"IN MY DAY WE HAD A RESPECT FOR POSSESSIONS."*

THE "THERE'S A CAR IN THERE SOMEWHERE" CAR

This is a vehicle over five years old, whose latest owner spends all his spare cash down at the motor accessory shop. Through all the fibreglass-modified panels, wheeltrims, strips, lights, horns and aerials, a skilled observer can sometimes identify what make of car it used to be.
STATEMENT : *"I'M PRETTY COOL, AREN'T I?"*

THE "GREAT OUTDOORS" CAR

This is usually one of those Japanese imitation Range Rovers with a covered spare wheel fixed on the back. Its distinctive features (four-wheel drive to cope with mountain roads, deserts, polar ice, etc.) are used mostly to negotiate the car park at Waitrose.
STATEMENT : *"I DON'T REALLY LIVE IN THE SUBURBS."*

THE "WE HAVEN'T REALLY GOT A CAR" CAR

This vehicle is refered to airly as "the heap" or "just something to get me from A to B." Lack of pride in its appearance and lack of interest in its mechanics are the distinguishing features of such car-owners. They somehow contrive to deny the car's existence even to the point of being able to join the anti-pollution lobby when the subject of petrol fumes comes up.

Favoured vehicles for such owners are old and, ideally, small. A Renault 4 fits the bill perfectly. So does a Volkswagen Beetle, a corrugated-iron Citroen 2CV or even an old Mini. A little Fiat 500 is another ·good one to disparage.
The seats of such cars are always covered in piles of papers and old coats, which have be moved to admit passengers.
STATEMENT : *"I'M FAR TOO INTERESTING A PERSON TO WORRY ABOUT SILLY OLD MATERIALISTIC THINGS LIKE CARS."*

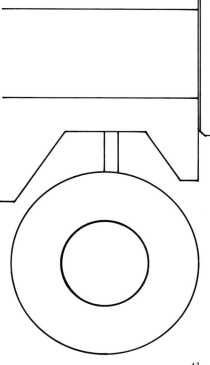

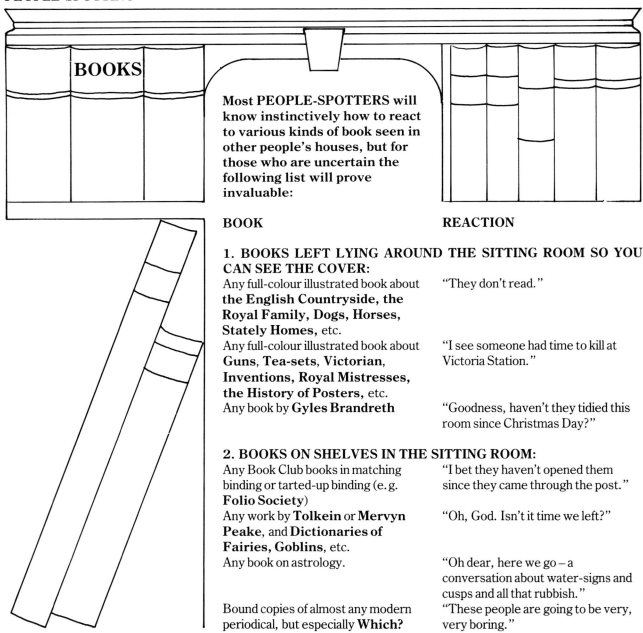

BOOKS

Most PEOPLE-SPOTTERS will know instinctively how to react to various kinds of book seen in other people's houses, but for those who are uncertain the following list will prove invaluable:

BOOK	REACTION

1. BOOKS LEFT LYING AROUND THE SITTING ROOM SO YOU CAN SEE THE COVER:

Any full-colour illustrated book about **the English Countryside, the Royal Family, Dogs, Horses, Stately Homes,** etc.	"They don't read."
Any full-colour illustrated book about **Guns, Tea-sets, Victorian, Inventions, Royal Mistresses, the History of Posters,** etc.	"I see someone had time to kill at Victoria Station."
Any book by **Gyles Brandreth**	"Goodness, haven't they tidied this room since Christmas Day?"

2. BOOKS ON SHELVES IN THE SITTING ROOM:

Any Book Club books in matching binding or tarted-up binding (e.g. **Folio Society**)	"I bet they haven't opened them since they came through the post."
Any work by **Tolkein** or **Mervyn Peake**, and **Dictionaries of Fairies, Goblins,** etc.	"Oh, God. Isn't it time we left?"
Any book on astrology.	"Oh dear, here we go – a conversation about water-signs and cusps and all that rubbish."
Bound copies of almost any modern periodical, but especially **Which?**	"These people are going to be very, very boring."

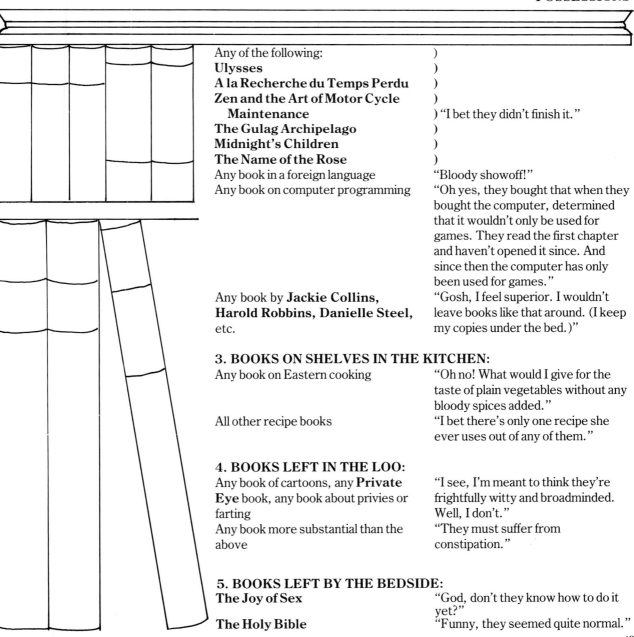

Any of the following:
Ulysses)
A la Recherche du Temps Perdu)
Zen and the Art of Motor Cycle)
   Maintenance) "I bet they didn't finish it."
The Gulag Archipelago)
Midnight's Children)
The Name of the Rose)

Any book in a foreign language — "Bloody showoff!"

Any book on computer programming — "Oh yes, they bought that when they bought the computer, determined that it wouldn't only be used for games. They read the first chapter and haven't opened it since. And since then the computer has only been used for games."

Any book by **Jackie Collins, Harold Robbins, Danielle Steel,** etc. — "Gosh, I feel superior. I wouldn't leave books like that around. (I keep my copies under the bed.)"

3. BOOKS ON SHELVES IN THE KITCHEN:

Any book on Eastern cooking — "Oh no! What would I give for the taste of plain vegetables without any bloody spices added."

All other recipe books — "I bet there's only one recipe she ever uses out of any of them."

4. BOOKS LEFT IN THE LOO:

Any book of cartoons, any **Private Eye** book, any book about privies or farting — "I see, I'm meant to think they're frightfully witty and broadminded. Well, I don't."

Any book more substantial than the above — "They must suffer from constipation."

5. BOOKS LEFT BY THE BEDSIDE:

The Joy of Sex — "God, don't they know how to do it yet?"

The Holy Bible — "Funny, they seemed quite normal."

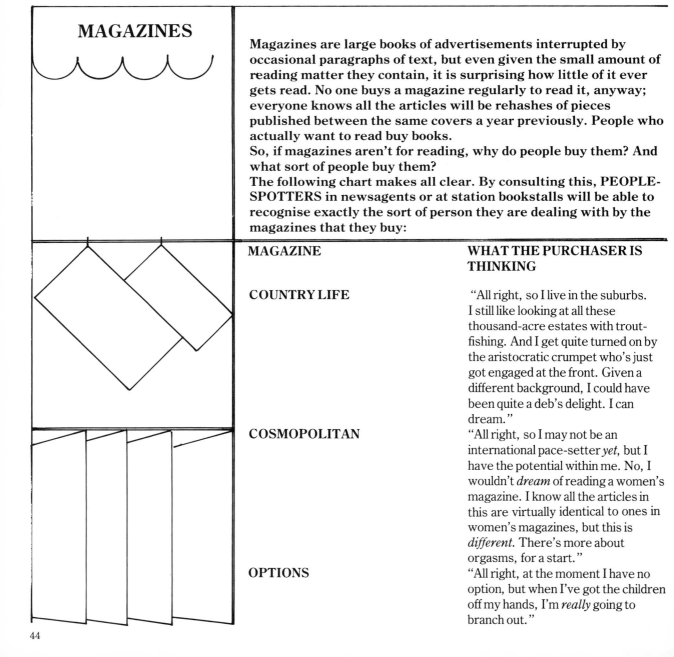

MAGAZINES

Magazines are large books of advertisements interrupted by occasional paragraphs of text, but even given the small amount of reading matter they contain, it is surprising how little of it ever gets read. No one buys a magazine regularly to read it, anyway; everyone knows all the articles will be rehashes of pieces published between the same covers a year previously. People who actually want to read buy books.

So, if magazines aren't for reading, why do people buy them? And what sort of people buy them?

The following chart makes all clear. By consulting this, PEOPLE-SPOTTERS in newsagents or at station bookstalls will be able to recognise exactly the sort of person they are dealing with by the magazines that they buy:

MAGAZINE	WHAT THE PURCHASER IS THINKING
COUNTRY LIFE	"All right, so I live in the suburbs. I still like looking at all these thousand-acre estates with trout-fishing. And I get quite turned on by the aristocratic crumpet who's just got engaged at the front. Given a different background, I could have been quite a deb's delight. I can dream."
COSMOPOLITAN	"All right, so I may not be an international pace-setter *yet*, but I have the potential within me. No, I wouldn't *dream* of reading a women's magazine. I know all the articles in this are virtually identical to ones in women's magazines, but this is *different*. There's more about orgasms, for a start."
OPTIONS	"All right, at the moment I have no option, but when I've got the children off my hands, I'm *really* going to branch out."

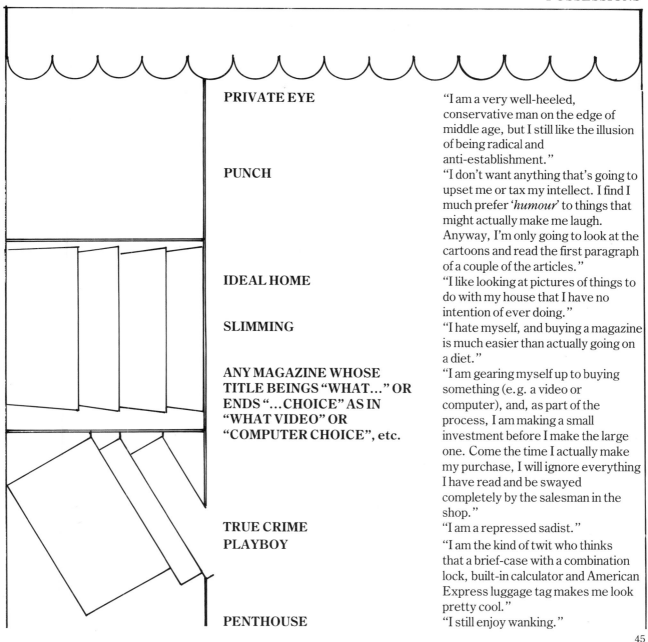

PRIVATE EYE

"I am a very well-heeled, conservative man on the edge of middle age, but I still like the illusion of being radical and anti-establishment."

PUNCH

"I don't want anything that's going to upset me or tax my intellect. I find I much prefer '*humour*' to things that might actually make me laugh. Anyway, I'm only going to look at the cartoons and read the first paragraph of a couple of the articles."

IDEAL HOME

"I like looking at pictures of things to do with my house that I have no intention of ever doing."

SLIMMING

"I hate myself, and buying a magazine is much easier than actually going on a diet."

ANY MAGAZINE WHOSE TITLE BEINGS "WHAT..." OR ENDS "...CHOICE" AS IN "WHAT VIDEO" OR "COMPUTER CHOICE", etc.

"I am gearing myself up to buying something (e.g. a video or computer), and, as part of the process, I am making a small investment before I make the large one. Come the time I actually make my purchase, I will ignore everything I have read and be swayed completely by the salesman in the shop."

TRUE CRIME

"I am a repressed sadist."

PLAYBOY

"I am the kind of twit who thinks that a brief-case with a combination lock, built-in calculator and American Express luggage tag makes me look pretty cool."

PENTHOUSE

"I still enjoy wanking."

PETS

The instinct in man to keep animals that serve no practical purpose is a bizarre one, but it is deeply-rooted, particularly in the British Isles. Like all other human activities, it reveals a lot about the people who do it.

Different types of owners identify themselves by the way they refer to their pets, and the following list of references will enable the keen PEOPLE-SPOTTER to recognise the kind of pet-owner he or she is dealing with:

"I GET A LOT MORE SENSE OUT OF HIM THAN I DO OUT OF MOST HUMAN BEINGS."

This is the voice of the misanthropic pet-owner, the person who finds animals easier to deal with than people. Frequently, though not always, this owner lives alone. The pet is most often a dog, though a cat – or even a budgie - can fill the role. The owner gets extremely annoyed if the pet shows affection to anyone else (but since the owner avoids contact with other people, this problem rarely arises).

"HE HATES BEING LEFT."

Like the above, this owner has an almost human relationship with the pet - again most frequently a dog or a cat. But here the attitude is not just one of bitterness to the outside world; it is also calculated to demonstrate the owner's tender nature. The pet is cosseted like a baby. The owner may live alone, but this is not always the case; this attitude to a pet is a very popular mutual pastime for married couples. It is also frequently used as a substitute for the CHILD EXCUSE (see page 60) to get out of almost anything.

"THE CHILDREN WOULDN'T GIVE US ANY PEACE UNTIL WE GOT HIM."

This line is usually spoken in a tone of some resentment by the person (most often the mother) left with the task of feeding the pet once the children have lost interest in it (i.e. in the second week of ownership). This animal can again be a dog or a cat, though with these it is possible for the exploited mother to develop some kind of workable relationship. The resentment in her tone will be at its strongest when the animal in question is one of those rodent-type creatures like hamsters, gerbils or guinea-pigs, which, though "everyone else at school has got one", have no appeal at all at any level. Her only comfort will be the knowledge that they don't live very long.

"WHEN HE GOES, WE WON'T GET ANOTHER ONE."

This can be the same kind of pet as the above, something that the children insisted on buying and whose every illness has been eagerly monitored ever since. It can, however, be part of a less baleful relationship, a cosy tolerance like that which arises in a long, but not particularly successful, marriage. Owners who make this statement are expressing a) their basic pragmatism, and b) the generosity of spirit which has kept them looking after their pet for so long.

"I DON'T KNOW IF YOU KNOW MUCH ABOUT THE SPECIES, BUT..."

This is the signal that the owner has got something really rare. The chances are that the person being addressed *doesn't* know much about the species, and is about to receive quite a lecture. It is also the warning sign that the owner is a "fancier". Fanciers' attitude to pets is different from most people's. Though they may feel incidental affection for the creatures, their main satisfaction is that of the collector. They are tuned into a bizarre subculture of specialist magazines and competitions whose standards are meaningless to anyone except another fancier. Though they may go for unusual dogs or cats, they are also liable to choose more exotic species – birds with a lot of redundant feathers or multicoloured fish in heated aquaria. Once they have identified this kind of pet-owner, PEOPLE-SPOTTERS are advised to make their excuses and leave as soon as possible.

"WE MUST LOOK OUR BEST, MUSTN'T WE?"

This identifies the "pet as accessory". Most frequently, it is a dog, and it is constantly being groomed and tarted up so that it matches the smartness of its owner. Not only is the animal treated as an accessory, it is also given its own accessories – flashy collars, little coats and so on. The most obvious of this species is the toy poodle, but there are plenty of others. Chihuahuas fit into this category, though quite what anyone can imagine having one of those on a lead does for their appearance is one of life's mysteries.

"DID WE TELL YOU THEIR NAMES?"

The only reason this kind of owner ever got pets was to give them witty names. Pairs of animals are favoured, so that the owner can indulge in such combinations as Fortnum and Mason, Laurel and Hardy, Donner and Blitzen, Morecambe and Wise, Ron and Eth, Bubble and Squeak, Little and Large, George and Ira, Castor and Pollux, Antony and Cleopatra, Hillard and Botting, Marks and Spencer, etc. As soon as each guest has been apprised of the names, the owner loses interest in the pets.

"I'VE ALWAYS HAD DOGS AROUND."

This is said by owners of public school background who were brought up in the country. Regardless of where they now live, they feel incomplete without a dog in the house. They tend to go for big ones, like Labradors, though one or two smaller breeds, Staffordshire bull-terriers or Jack Russells for example, are also suitable. These owners are not overtly sentimental about the animals, speaking much of "discipline" and even using the imperative "sir!" In company, they enjoy shouting at their pets, to demonstrate their iron control. They feel it's important that their children should grow up with dogs, as if this conveyed some unspecified moral advantage.

"HE'S A ONE-MAN DOG."

This is frequently said by the above owners, though it is not exclusive to them. It is a remark meant to hint at some almost mystical bond that the owner has with his pet, some mysterious extra dimension to his personality. Woe betide the person who proves that the dog is just as friendly and obedient with someone else!

"I LIKE A DOG TO BE A DOG."

This may also be said by the "I'VE ALWAYS HAD DOGS AROUND" owner, and it is used to justify having a particularly big and brutal specimen. The remark is much favoured by people with Alsatians, and is always meant to impart some of the dog's *machismo* to its owner.

"HE'S A RANDY OLD DEVIL, AREN'T YOU?"

This can be addressed to a dog or a tom-cat, either of which is reputed to wreak havoc among the females of the district. Like the above, it is always said to imply that, given the chance, the owner would have the same sexual dimension.

"OH, HE'S A BIT OF EVERYTHING, AREN'T YOU?"

This is addressed to a mongrel, and almost always accompanied by an affectionate ruffling of the hair on the dog's head. It is also always meant to carry the implication that the owner is a lovable, happy-go-lucky sort of person.

"HE'S A GREAT FOOL, AREN'T YOU?"

This is also usually accompanied by a ruffling of the head, though the animal can be a dog or a cat. The animal's soppiness, to which the remark refers, is assiduously encouraged, to point up the superiority of its owner.

"I'M NOT SURE HOW MANY IT IS NOW…"

This is most often said by cat-owners, and it's the sign of a household overrun by the animals. Each one has a history – it was going to be drowned, it was mistreated by its previous owner, it just turned up on the doorstep, it was one of *her* litter and I just hadn't the heart to give it away, etc. – and it is difficult for the visitor to avoid hearing that history. The line is usually spoken by a woman, as she scoops one of the cats out of a chair to make room for her guest, and is always calculated to give an impression of her slight scattiness and warm heart.

"YOU KNOW HOW IT IS WHEN YOU'VE GOT ANIMALS…"

This remarks is always accompanied by a disarming shrug. Like the above, it means that the house is overrun by animals, but it also means that's why everything's such a mess. Chewed rugs, scratched armchair covers, a legacy of dog-hairs from anything you sit on, and an unwholesomely damp smell are the distinguishing marks of the home of such an owner.

PROHIBITIONS AND ESSENTIALS

People get extremely vehement on the subject of what they will and won't allow in their houses. PEOPLE-SPOTTERS should always be listening out for statements which take the form "WE WON'T HAVE——" IN THE HOUSE" or "WE ALWAYS HAVE——", because such remarks are made with the intention of emphasising the speaker's wonderful qualities, as outlined below:

(N.B. There is nothing wrong with any of the attitudes expressed it is only the fact that people make such a point of drawing one's attention to them that is offensive.)

"WE WON'T HAVE A TELEVISION IN THE HOUSE."
("We are deeply wonderful people dedicated to the old-fashioned values of conversation and family life. The fact that our children are shunned in the playground because they don't understand the games that all the other children are playing is just one of the penalties of being the offspring of such truly wonderful people.")

"WE WON'T HAVE A COMPUTER IN THE HOUSE."
("This is not because we, in common with most families, would have absolutely no use for a computer. It's because we are confused and frightened by modern technology, and don't want to be shown up by our kids.")

"WE WON'T HAVE TOY GUNS IN THE HOUSE."
("This is because we are truly wonderful peace-loving people who fear that playing with guns will breed habits of violence in our children. In other words, we have no faith in their strength of character or discrimination.")

"WE WON'T HAVE CONVENIENCE FOODS IN THE HOUSE."
("We have a lot of time on our hands.")

"WE WON'T HAVE CHEWING GUM IN THE HOUSE."
("We retain our parents' values that chewing is *common*. As a result, our front garden is littered with little bits of half-used chewing gum spat out by our children as they come home from school.")

"WE WON'T HAVE WHITE BREAD IN THE HOUSE."
("This demonstrates our wonderful concern for our health. It also means that no one talks at breakfast because we're all too busy chewing.")

"WE WON'T HAVE WHITE SUGAR IN THE HOUSE."
("This again shows our wonderful concern for health and our bold resistance to the poisons of modern civilisation. The fact that there is white sugar in almost all the food that we buy is one which we choose to ignore.")

"WE WOULDN'T HAVE A MEMBER OF THE NATIONAL FRONT IN THE HOUSE."

("We are wonderfully liberal people. Since we don't know anyone who belongs to the National Front, it is not difficult for us to make such pronouncements.")

"WE ALWAYS HAVE LOTS OF BOOKS AROUND."

("We are wonderfully literate, so superior to the television generation.")

"WE ALWAYS HAVE RADIO THREE ON."

("We are wonderfully cultured and sophisticated.")

"WE ALWAYS HAVE RECYCLED LAVATORY PAPER."

("We are wonderfully responsible people, permanently conscious of our duties to the ecology of Planet Earth.")

"WE ALWAYS HAVE ORGANICALLY GROWN VEGETABLES."

("Not only are we wonderfully responsible, we are also wonderfully aware of the hazards posed to our health by modern civilisation.")

"WE ALWAYS HAVE FREE-RANGE EGGS."

("Not only are we wonderfully responsible and wonderfully aware of the hazards posed to our health by modern civilisation, we are also wonderfully concerned about the rights of animals.")

"WE ALWAYS HAVE LOTS OF OTHER PEOPLE'S CHILDREN IN THE HOUSE."

("We are a wonderfully open, warm and loving family. We welcome everyone, particularly, we like to think, children whose parents do not perhaps give them as much love, attention and stimulation as our children receive. And we feel that children who do come to our house leave with their lives perhaps a little enriched by the experience.")

"WE ALWAYS SEEM TO HAVE SOMEONE WHO HAS JUST BROKEN UP A LONG-TERM RELATIONSHIP IN THE HOUSE."

("We are wonderfully giving and sympathetic people. Such people are attracted to us, because we understand. We are attracted to them, because they make us feel wonderfully superior.")

"WE ALWAYS SEEM TO HAVE SOMEONE FROM ABROAD IN THE HOUSE."

The someone from abroad should be depressed and – ideally – black.

("We are wonderfully giving, sympathetic and tolerant people. Foreigners make us feel wonderfully superior.")

PEOPLE AS POSSESSIONS

The Middle Class, as well as all its inanimate possessions, also likes to own people. It gains reassurance from being able to talk of certain people as "my" whatever; this gives a feeling of historical continuity and helps to alleviate the sense of rootlessness which is so much a characteristic of the species. Here is a list of the main people the Middle Class like to claim as possessions:

"MY SOLICITOR"

An essential weapon in the armoury. Though chiefly used for conveyancing and drawing up wills, he is often jocularly referred to in cases of imagined insult *("Ooh, I'll have to get my solicitor on to that…")*. Those who wish to be really cool will ensure that they have a female solicitor and make many gratuitous references to *"her"*.

"MY ACCOUNTANT"

The self-employed refer to this figure constantly, in fact as constantly as they harp on the tax problems brought about by their amazing success. But people on P.A.Y.E. also find it useful to be able to drop in conversation mysterious remarks such as, *"Well, I'd have to check it out with my accountant…"*

"MY BUILDER"

This mythic figure has nothing to do with the sort of builders everyone else encounters. This is the one who will appear at a moment's notice to fix problems around the house and charge virtually nothing. *"It could have been a bit nasty, but I got on to my builder and he came round straight away and…!"* No one ever actually sees this paragon, nor will its owner ever give its phone number. ("MY BUILDER" is frequently one of a set which includes "MY DECORATOR", "MY PLUMBER", "MY ELECTRICIAN", "MY BLOKE WHO SORTS OUT THE CAR", etc.)

"MY STYLIST"

The only person who understands the speaker's hair.

"MY ANALYST"

Constant references to this figure never let the listener forget that he or she is dealing with someone of exceptional sensitivity.

"MY GURU"

Used randomly to add mystery to the speaker.

"MY CONSULTANT"

For all other medical personnel as possessions, see the section on HEALTH.

7 WORK

The ever-present threat of redundancy has added another to their growing list of **Anxieties**, but work still remains at the centre of Middle Class thinking. Though, in discussions of unemployment they are frequently heard to remark that **"people exist as people and shouldn't be thought of just according to what job they have"** or **"there's so much more to life than work – it's so much more important to be a fully developed human being"**, they don't actually believe this.

Work, after all, provides money, and it is money that fuels the Middle Class life-style. Money buys the clothes, the homes, the possessions with which Middle Class man disguises himself. And a comfortable amount of money is required to cushion the constant Middle Class complaint that **"we're terribly hard-up – we just don't know how we're going to manage."**

But work doesn't just bring in the loot; it also gives rein to those two other Middle Class characteristics, **Aspiration** and **Disappointment**. Though they frequently and deviously avoid admitting it, members of the Middle Class are always trying to **Do Better, Get Promoted, Get On, Be A Success**. When these **Aspirations** fail, they have the opportunity to wallow in **Disappointment**.

Work can also be a fine focus for **Guilt**. Middle Class men can feel guilty about their success, guilty about their failure, guilty about how much money the earn, guilty about how little, guilty about how commercial the work they do is, guilty about the fact that their work makes them feel guilty.

Middle Class working women can feel all this and, if they happen to be working mothers, can add a whole range of refinements to which masculine guilt cannot aspire.

Work, then, is a subject on which readers of this book should be properly informed, and a perusal of the ensuing pages will prove invaluable in the categorisation by occupation of the species which is the PEOPLE-SPOTTER'S study.

When people are categorised by their work, there are seven main types that qualified PEOPLE-SPOTTERS should be able to identify. They are as follows:

1. PEOPLE WHO DO THINGS,
2. PEOPLE WHO MAKE THINGS,
3. PEOPLE WHO MAKE OTHER PEOPLE DO THINGS,
4. PEOPLE WHO DO THINGS TO THINGS OTHER PEOPLE MAKE,
5. PEOPLE WHO STOP PEOPLE DOING THINGS,
6. PEOPLE WHO KEEP THINGS THE WAY THEY ARE,
and
7. PEOPLE WHO DON'T DO A LOT.

These types can be labelled respectively as:

1. INITIATORS,
2. CONSTRUCTORS,
3. FIXERS,
4. SERVICERS,
5. OBSTRUCTORS,
6. PERPETUATORS,
and
7. PASSENGERS.

Though not all professions fit neatly into only one category (for example, though most country solicitors are PASSENGERS, not all are), these descriptions are a very useful method of defining the sort of work people do. It is usually simple to recognise from people's conversation which category they fit into, but the following notes may prove useful to the novice PEOPLE-SPOTTERS:

1. INITIATORS (PEOPLE WHO DO THINGS)

These are the original thinkers, the ones who introduce new ideas and actually change things. Though they occur in every sort of work, they are so rare that PEOPLE-SPOTTERS are advised not to waste their time looking for them.

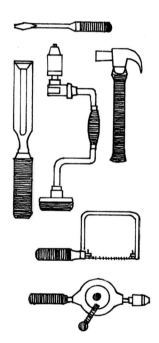

2. CONSTRUCTORS (PEOPLE WHO MAKE THINGS)

Since PEOPLE-SPOTTERS are, by definition, Middle Class, they are unlikely to meet any of the CONSTRUCTORS who work in the manufacturing industry (unless perhaps their cleaning lady's husband comes to the house to pick her up after his night shift). Anyway, the British manufacturing industry is dwindling at such a rate, there soon won't be anyone left to meet.

The kind of CONSTRUCTORS PEOPLE-SPOTTERS *are* likely to meet usually have some vague connection with the Arts. Anyone who calls himself a "craftsman" fits into this category and, since everything that doesn't come off an assembly-line is nowadays reckoned to be "craftsman-made", that covers a great range. (Makers of dung-coloured pottery; carvers of wooden toys that grandparents buy for children who won't play with them because what they really want are plastic spin-offs from the latest movie; and well-heeled girls with knitting machines who sell woolly jumpers on stalls in Covent Garden, all fit into the category.)

Actors, writers and television producers would also describe themselves as CONSTRUCTORS, though this claim is open to dispute.

Identifying remarks PEOPLE-SPOTTERS should listen out for from CONSTRUCTORS include the following:

1. "When I'm working, the creative process takes over…"
2. "Of course I always use traditional tools… well, except for the heavy work, I use power tools for that…"
3. "Of course I don't do it for the money…"

3. FIXERS

These are the most resilient type. Any sort of agent is obviously a FIXER. So are stockbrokers, solicitors, factory foremen, Production Managers, etc., etc., etc. The category covers a wide range of effort and commitment. Some FIXERS show sufficient originality almost to qualify as INITIATORS, while others (e.g. most Estate Agents - let's face it, nobody sells houses, they sell themselves) are pretty well PASSENGERS.

PEOPLE-SPOTTERS will be able to recognise FIXERS by their use of the following sentences:

1. "Of course I would love to accept what you're offering but I'm afraid my client…"
2. "Of course I have no personal axe to grind; I'm just recommending the best that's available…"
3. "Leave it with me"

4. SERVICERS

This is the fastest-growing category in the country. As quickly as manufacturing CONSTRUCTORS vanish, they are replaced by new SERVICERS. Anyone who sells, repairs or transports things fits into this group. It is unfortunate that their name carries overtones of willing assistance, since this is something they rarely demonstrate.

The simplest way for PEOPLE-SPOTTERS to recognise SERVICERS is by a pessimistically jutting lower lip and the use of the following sentences:

1. "It can't be done."
2. "You've been having a go at it yourself, haven't you?"
3. "It's going to cost you."

 *1.*
 *2.*
 *3.*

5. OBSTRUCTORS (PEOPLE WHO STOP PEOPLE DOING THINGS)

There are two main sorts of OBSTRUCTORS, those who wear uniforms, and those who sit in offices. The first type obviously includes policemen, park attendants and little men who interrupt the last movements of symphonies because it's time the hall closed; and the second, local council planning officers, bank managers, building society managers and tax inspectors.

PEOPLE-SPOTTERS should be alert for the following utterances:

1. *"No."*
2. *"But if we let everyone go ahead and do what you suggest, well, it'd be anarchy, wouldn't it?"*
3. *"I'm sorry."*

(N.B. This last, always accompanied by a shake of the head is of course a blatant lie.)

6. PERPETUATORS

Into this category come most of the established professions.

PERPETUATORS abound in any institution where seniority is more highly valued than original thought (e.g. the Law, Accountancy, the Civil Service, the Armed Forces, Parliament, etc.)

PEOPLE-SPOTTERS will find that the following statements help them to identify the speaker as a PERPETUATOR:

1. *"Well, what we've done when this situation has arisen in the past is..."*
2. *"Well, you've got to have standards, haven't you?"*
3. *"Now I'm as open to new ideas as the next man, but..."*

7. PASSENGERS

There are specimens of this type in every walk of life, and they all share the knack of always finding someone who will carry them. The boss run by his secretary is an obvious example, but there are plenty of other manifestations, The category includes most executives whose title includes the word "Organiser" or "Co-ordinator", all British Rail porters, and, of course, the majority of people who appear on television chat-shows.

N.B. It is important to make the distinction between an UNWILLING PASSENGER (e.g. one of the unemployed) and a DELIBERATE PASSENGER (e.g. an Executive Producer in television).

Sentences PEOPLE-SPOTTERS should listen out for include the following:

1. *"Yes, I'm keeping very busy."*
2. *"I always try to take an overall view, not to get bogged down in details."*
3. *"Well, thank you. It's really great to be on the show."*

ELBOW LINES

In every area of business people lose jobs. Redundancy is fast becoming a leisure activity to rival television-viewing. There are, however, ways of losing jobs which do not involve leaving a company. Any number of demotions and downgradings are available for the executive whose face doesn't fit, and the bigger the organisation, the greater the area of grass out to which employees can be put.

But downgrading is rarely described as such – least of all by the person downgraded. PEOPLE-SPOTTERS, however, need suffer no confusion. When hearing someone talk of "a new direction at work" or "an exciting new challenge", they should be able to recognise instantly whether or not this is a polite way of describing "the elbow". All they have to do is refer to the following chart:

REMARK	REAL MEANING
"I've been assigned to a special project."	"They'll do anything to keep me out of the day-to-day running of the Department."
"I'm doing a survey on the way the Department is run."	AS ABOVE
"I'm joining the Staff Training Department."	"I'm utterly useless."
"I have been made Head of Staff Training."	"I am utterly useless but I'm so senior that they've had to give me a title to stop me from making embarrassing applications for jobs that really matter."
"I have been made Head of Personnel."	AS ABOVE
"I feel it's time I got back to the creative side of the business."	"I made a hash of being Head of Department."
IN TELEVISION: "I am going to concentrate on independent production."	"I have been chucked out."
"I am going to concentrate on my writing."	AS ABOVE
IN POLITICS: "I'm taking the Northern Ireland portfolio."	"The Prime Minister hates me."

8

PARENTHOOD

Children provide a wonderful focus for those four Middle Class characteristics: **Aspiration**, **Disappointment**, **Guilt** and **Anxiety**.

Since the Middle Class is always by definition in a state of flux, Middle Class parents never dare to want just the same for their children as they have had themselves. Their insecurity is so strong that they always want their children to **Do Better** – to have more social poise, to be better educated, to marry better, to get better jobs, to make more money. Those are the great **Aspirations**; when they are not realised, **Disappointment** sets in. Children also provide wonderful opportunities for **Guilt**. Before actually breeding, Middle Class parents can spend years agonising about whether this is a fit world into which to bring children. Then, once pregnancy is under way, much time can be spent weighing and feeling guilty about the rival claims of mechanised hospital delivery and Natural Childbirth.

When the children have actually arrived, it's open season for **Guilt**. Are we bringing them up properly? Are we insufficiently loving, so that they will grow up to be psychopaths? Are we too loving, and will they therefore be incapable in later life of building up mature relationships of their own? Are we too strict with them? Are we too indulgent? The list of **Guilt**-triggers is infinite.

Guilt also prompts much of the **Anxiety**. Francis Bacon described having children as having "hostages to fortune", and no one is more aware of this situation than the Middle Class parent, who is in a state of constant paranoia, in momentary anticipation of fortune's latest ransom demand. Are the children all right crossing the road? Are they safe on bicycles? Have they got nits? Are they all right mixing with that crowd from school they go around with? Are the girls getting pregnant? Are the boys getting the girls pregnant? Are they on drugs? Worst of all, are they becoming *common*? These questions and many others help to keep the Middle Class parent in that lather of **Anxiety** on which the species masochistically thrives. But children are not without their advantages, as can be seen overleaf.

THE CHILD EXCUSE

Though children bring their inconveniences, they can also prove of great use to their parents in a variety of ways. Their usefulness starts from the moment of conception. A pregnant woman is not expected to take on too much *because of her condition*, and skilled parents can turn their children into a permanent *condition* which lets them off a great many social responsibilities. They always have a morally impeccable alibi, which gives them a distinct advantage over the childless, who have to be much more inventive in their lies and excuses.

Here are some of the most common uses of the Child Excuse (along with the appropriate line for each occasion):

TO GET OUT OF AN INVITATION TO ANY SOCIAL FUNCTION
"Oh, we'd love to, but we've got problems with babysitters..."

TO GET OUT OF AN INVITATION TO ANY SOCIAL FUNCTION AT ABOUT HALF AN HOUR'S NOTICE:
"I'm sorry, one of the kids has developed something..."

TO LEAVE ANY SOCIAL FUNCTION EARLY:
"Sorry, but we promised the babysitter..."

TO EXCUSE BORING CONVERSATION:
"Not having spoken to anyone over five all day, I ..."

TO JUSTIFY DOING NO HOUSEWORK:
"The children make such a mess..."

TO JUSTIFY LOOKING A MESS:
"By the time I've got the children looking respectable..."

TO JUSTIFY BUYING AN EXPENSIVE DRESS:
"Quite honestly, after a day with the kids, I feel I need..."

TO JUSTIFY EARLY DRINKING:
"Quite honestly, after a day with the kids, I feel I need..."

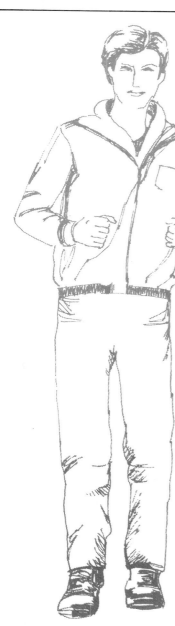

TO JUSTIFY WATCHING RUBBISH ON TELEVISION:
"All I'm fit for by the time I've got the children to bed..."

TO JUSTIFY WATCHING TOP OF THE POPS:
"Well, I have to keep up with what the children are into..."

TO JUSTIFY GOING TO SEE REALLY BAD FILMS:
"The children were set on it and someone had to go along..."

TO JUSTIFY BUYING A HOME COMPUTER:
"It's for the children, mainly. You see, at school they..."

TO EXCUSE TELLING A BAD JOKE:
"One of the kids came back from school with this story about..."

TO EXCUSE CAREER FAILURE (FOR A WOMAN):
"But then the children came along and..."

TO EXCUSE CAREER FAILURE (FOR A MAN):
"And, basically, I wanted to spend more time with the children..."

TO EXCUSE NOT TAKING UP A NEW CHALLENGE:
"But that'd mean the children changing schools and..."

*TO GAIN MORAL ASCENDANCY OVER SOMEONE MORE
SUCCESSFUL:*
"But then of course you haven't got children..."

TO LIMIT RESPONSIBILITY IN AN EXTRAMARITAL AFFAIR:
"I tell you, if it weren't for the children..."

TO JUSTIFY STAYING MARRIED:
"I tell you, if it weren't for the children..."

TO JUSTIFY ANY BAD DECISION:
"We did it for the children..."

TO GET OUT OF ANYTHING:
"We have to think of the children..."

EDUCATION

Education is the great Middle Class obsession, and PEOPLE-SPOTTERS should be able to recognise educational attitudes through the many misleading layers in which they are shrouded. As with anything else which the Middle Class regards as an *ISSUE* (e.g. sex, politics, charity, diet, family, marriage, life, etc.) education gives rise to a great deal of *GUILT* and *HEARTSEARCHING*. The Middle Class distinguishing features of *ASPIRATION* and *DISAPPOINTMENT* are grossly exaggerated once their children become involved. Though, if asked, they would deny it, the hope is always cherished in Middle Class bosoms that the next generation is going to do better than the current one, and Middle Class parents have all been brainwashed into the belief that *EDUCATION IS THE KEY TO SUCCESS*. Any pronouncement on the subject is therefore made against this background. The following pronouncements on education have been translated for the benefit of would-be PEOPLE-SPOTTERS:

PRONOUNCEMENT	REAL MEANING	
"His teachers say he's got a lot of artistic talent."	"He's not doing very well."	40%
"His teachers say he's got a lot of personality."	"He is disruptive in class."	25%
"He's doing very well at sport."	"He's doing very badly at everything else."	50%
"He mixes with a good cross-section at school."	"We feel socially superior to most of the other children and parents at the school."	80%
"He seems to have a different voice for when he talks to his friends."	"His vowels are appalling."	20%
"We've always favoured private education."	"We want our children to have nice vowels."	99%
"We really aren't that bothered about where our kids go to school."	"We are lying."	100%
"We really aren't that bothered about where our kids go to school but our parents feel strongly about private education."	"Our parents are paying the fees."	99%

"And if we have to miss out on a few foreign holidays and what-have-you, well…"	"God, all those years of penury stretching ahead!"	15%
"We believe in choice."	"We are going to educate our children privately."	88%
"But if you do it for one, you can't *not* do it for the others."	"We are going to educate our children through the State system."	50%
"We'd certainly recommend you to do the same as us and put your kids into the local comprehensive."	"If enough Middle Class families put families put their kids into the local comprehensive, then it'll be just like having private education without paying - won't it?"	75%
"The universities are really crying out for candidates from the comprehensives."	"We read that somewhere and we hope to God it's true."	90%
"At the primary level, the State system is fine - it's after that…"	"We are hoping to get by with giving our kids all the advantages of private education and only paying for part of it."	87%
"I went through the State system and it didn't do me any harm."	*"Did* it?"	50%
"I went through public school and it didn't do me any harm."	*"Did* it?"	45%
"I was a boarder and it didn't do me any harm."	*"Did* it?"	40%
"As parents, we're very involved in what goes on at the school."	"The teachers duck every time they see us coming."	25%
"We won't hear a word against the comprehensive - it's got him a place at university."	*"WHEW!"*	96%
"Of course we're sorry he didn't make it to university, but we still feel he got a great deal out of private education."	*"SHIT!* All that money!"	15%

SCALE OF VALUES

Middle Class parents have a very rigid scale of values with regard to their children. PEOPLE-SPOTTERS should be aware of the following main articles of belief:

1. Middle Class parents would rather their child was described by its teacher as *"having behavioural problems"* than as *"being a bloody little nuisance"*.

2. Middle Class parents would rather their children contracted measles than nits.

3. Middle Class parents would rather that their children were nice to their (i.e. the parents') friends than to their own (i. e. the children's) friends.

4. Middle Class parents would rather their children smoked marijuana in private than chewed gum in the street.

5. Middle Class parents would rather their teenage daughters were madly promiscuous but on the pill than madly in love and pregnant.

6. Middle Class parents would rather their teenage daughters became rich men's mistresses than suddenly had burning vocations to become nuns.

7. Middle Class parents would rather their teenage sons smashed up other people's cars than smashed up their parents' cars.

8. Middle Class parents would rather their children were arrested for drug offences than for shoplifting.

9. Middle Class parents would rather their children married when they were over 25 than when they were under 20.

10. Middle Class parents would rather their children had bad morals than bad vowels.

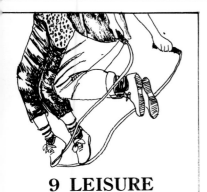

9 LEISURE

As in all its other activities, the Middle Class approaches Leisure as a public affair. The aim is not just to do something, but to be *seen* to do something. Relaxation is not much use if no one knows that you're relaxing.

So even what seems like the most antisocial and private (and, incidentally, the most popular) of leisure activities, television-watching, always takes on a public dimension. Though the actual watching may be done in private, the important element in the exercise is the ensuing conversation about what has been watched. This conversation is rarely an intellectual discussion pursuing the points raised by individual programmes; it is usually a form of assessment. By hearing what programmes other people watch, and what their attitudes to them are, the member of the Middle Class stands a chance of reaching that feeling of superiority to which he or she constantly aspires. The reading of books, too, is indulged not just for pleasure, but as a step to social superiority. Books exist only for their titles to be dropped in conversation, to be quoted from to point up a listener's ignorance, or to demonstrate the breadth of the reader's humanity. The superiority aspired to is not necessarily intellectual; indeed, the habit of reading rubbish is frequently alluded to to add a new and unexpected dimension to the speaker's image.

Sport, too, is a public activity. Again, there is no point in doing it if nobody knows about it. The few who have the ability make their mark by being good at sport, but incompetence does not disqualify others from giving out signals about themselves by the games that they play.

A Middle Class holiday is also a public statement. It cannot exist in a vacuum; it only becomes real when people other than the participants know about it. This explains the prevalence of postcards sent from holiday locations. Their aim is not to communicate information, merely to ensure that the recipient is not allowed to forget that the sender is on holiday.

All of these leisure activities obviously offer a rich field of investigation for the aspiring PEOPLE-SPOTTER, and in the ensuing pages tips will be given on how to conduct that investigation.

TELEVISION

Since television-watching is the most popular leisure activity in the country, it's not surprising that people talk about it a great deal. Acute PEOPLE-SPOTTERS, however, would not be so naive as to take what is said on the subject at face value. For ready reference, here are the REAL MEANINGS of some of the most common PRONOUNCEMENTS about television:

PRONOUNCEMENT	REAL MEANING
"There's nothing on television these days."	"But that doesn't stop me from sitting in front of it for hours."
"Television has killed the art of conversation."	"Not that I was ever much good at it, anyway."
"Did you see that programme last night about…?"	"Television has killed the art of conversation."
"The television happened to be on last night and …"	"I had switched the television on last night and …"
"I think public access television is incredibly important."	"I think public access television is incredibly boring."
"If I had to choose, I'd much sooner give up the television than listening to the radio."	"But I still spend much more time watching television than listening to the radio."
"I only watch documentaries."	"I am lying."
"I only watch arts programmes."	"I am lying."
"I've never watched ITV."	"I am lying."
"Television always does costume drama well."	"Television occasionally does costume drama well."

"I would go and watch sport live, but the fact is that you do see a lot more on television." / "I would never go and watch sport live. The fact is that I am totally idle."

"My ideal Saturday night is a few cans of beer and *Match of the Day*." / "The magic has gone out of my marriage."

"The best programme of the week for me is *Panorama*." / "I am showing off."

"The best programme of the week for me is *Game for a Laugh*." / "I am educationally subnormal."

"I watch *Dallas* for laughs." / "No, I don't. I watch it for exactly the same reason as all those people I'm trying to be patronisingly superior to — because I enjoy it."

"I wouldn't dream of watching *Coronation Street*." / "Because I'm afraid of getting hooked on it."

"I think *Little and Large* are very funny." / "I have no sense of humour."

"I always enjoy *Terry and June*." / "I have no sense of humour."

"*The Two Ronnies* are very sharp." / "*The Two Ronnies* were very sharp."

"My children don't want to watch *Grange Hill*." / "I won't let my children watch *Grange Hill*."

"Most of the old movies on television are really wonderful." / "Some of the old movies on television are really wonderful."

"Television brings the world into my living-room." / "Television brings me into my living-room."

TELEVISION STATISTICS

Because television is such an important influence on people, it is essential that PEOPLE-SPOTTERS should be aware of the way the medium operates, and particularly of its use of statistical information and the graphical representation of that information. (Besides, habitual readers of books of this kind feel cheated if they get this far in without seeing some meaningless graphics.)

USE OF SLICE-OF-CAKE GRAPHICS

At one time these were a rarity, which might be found in programmes of Budget analysis, news reports on government spending, etc., but over the last ten years their spread has reached epidemic proportions, and there remain very few programmes with any informational content which do not use them - as explained in the adjacent diagrams and the key below:

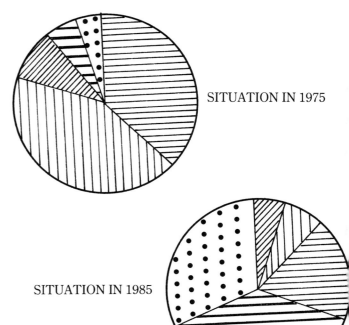

SITUATION IN 1975

SITUATION IN 1985

 PROGRAMMES RELYING ON OLD-FASHIONED METHODS OF RELAYING INFORMATION (i.e. SPEECH)

 PROGRAMMES WHICH OCCASIONALLY USE SLICE-OF-CAKE GRAPHICS TO REINFORCE A POINT

 PROGRAMMES WHICH USE RATHER TOO MANY SLICE-OF-CAKE GRAPHICS

 PROGRAMMES WHICH USE SLICE-OF-CAKE GRAPHICS AT EVERY CONCEIVABLE OPPORTUNITY

 PROGRAMMES WHICH USE SLICE-OF-CAKE GRAPHICS WHEN THERE IS ABSOLUTELY NO CALL FOR THEM

LITERARY ADJECTIVES

The adjectival use of writers' names has a long history. Describing a situation as "Pinteresque" or "like something out of P.G.Wodehouse" is an overused shorthand which remains popular because,

a) it is evocative of the world created by those writers, and,

b) it demonstrates how well-read the speaker is.

The trouble with such usages is that they get misapplied or used so approximately that they lose much of their strength (and grossly misrepresent the writers concerned). Also, like old school ties, they get appropriated by people whose education gives them no right to their use. Specially for PEOPLE-SPOTTERS, here is a list of writers commonly used as adjectives, together with their current meanings:

AMIS, MARTIN:
Nasty, dirty. A city street in the fourth week of a dustmen's strike would be described as "very Martin Amis".

AYCKBOURN, ALAN:
Boringly domestic. Any conversation about ceiling tiles comes under the heading of "Pure Ayckbourn".

BECKETT, SAMUEL:
Pertaining to a tramp. Being asked to spare 50p for a cup of tea is "a very Samuel Beckett experience".

BETJEMAN, JOHN:
Innocuously charming. Gymkhanas are automatically "Betjeman"; so are cream teas, seaside picnics, grass tennis-courts, teddy bears, bakelite wirelesses, etc.

BRECHT, BERTOLT:
Still used in the form "Brechtian" to describe any theatrical performance the speaker doesn't understand.

BRONTË, CHARLOTTE, EMILY, ETC:
Windswept. Frequently in the coining "Brontëesque", it is nowadays used to describe anything from a rainstorm to a hairstyle.

BROOKNER, ANITA:
Lonely (of a woman). As in the following exchange:
A: "What's the matter with you?"
B: "Oh, I don't know. I'm just feeling a bit Anita Brookner."

BYRON, GEORGE GORDON, LORD:
Windswept (cf. BRONTE). Used in the form "Byronic", to describe a pop singer's hairstyle.

COOPER, JILLY:
See BETJEMAN, JOHN.

COWARD, NOËL:	Pertaining to the Thirties. Very rarely now used to describe epigrams or situations, but frequently to describe blazers, white flannels, cigarette-holders, cocktail shakers, etc., usually in the slightly mocking formula, "Oh, very Noël Coward".
DAHL, ROALD:	Ominous, unnerving. A telephone that rings with no one at the other end might be said to be "extremely Roald Dahl".
DICKENS, CHARLES:	Old, outdated. Used in the form "Dickensian" to describe things rather than people, e.g. "...and the central heating is positively Dickensian!"
FITZGERALD, SCOTT:	Failed, frequently because of drink. Any yesteryear whizzkid is described, with a hopeless shrug, as "pure Scott Fitzgerald". Also used interchangably with COWARD, NOËL, to describe cocktail shakers, etc.
FRANCIS, DICK:	Pertaining to horses.
GREENE, GRAHAM:	Gloomy, dull, overcast. This usage is now so common that it's only a matter of time before the weathermen start using it.
HEMINGWAY, ERNEST:	Rugged and tickly. Used nowadays only to refer to pullovers and beards.
JONG, ERICA:	Sexually adventurous (of a woman). It is, however, only used to describe an unattractive woman given to talking embarrassingly about her promiscuity.
LAWRENCE, D.H.:	In the open air. Used by couples who have just made love out of doors to describe what they've done.
LEE, LAURIE:	Charmingly primitive. Used in antique shops by couples looking at pestles and mortars, stone hot-water-bottles, floral chamber-pots, etc.
MURDOCH, IRIS:	Complex (of a relationship). Any male divorcee living with his ex-wife's brother, for example, would be said to be "straight out of Iris Murdoch".
ORWELL, GEORGE:	Impersonal (of a public official). As in "Honestly, the people in that Post Office are like something out of Orwell."
PINTER, HAROLD:	Quirky, odd. Usually used in the form "Pinteresque" to describe a conversation with anyone more reticent than oneself. Also can be applied to any interior that is insufficiently lit.
POWELL, ANTHONY:	This adjective is used to describe an encounter with anyone one has not seen since school or university. As in, "Guess who I bumped into? It was very Anthony Powell."
PROUST, MARCEL:	In the form "Proustian" this word is applied to any memory, as in the following exchange: A: "I was just thinking about my old maths teacher." B: "Oh, very Proustian." Also used to describe most kinds of cakes and biscuits.
STOPPARD, TOM:	Witty. Anyone who makes a pun, however feeble, is likely to have it acclaimed as "worthy of Stoppard". Anyone who makes two puns will be hailed as "positively Stoppardian".

THOMAS, DYLAN:	Drunk.
TROLLOPE, ANTHONY:	Pertaining to the church. The adjective "Trollopian" is used by tourists to describe a cathedral close or an elderly vicar.
UPDIKE, JOHN:	Given to suburban wife-swapping.
WILDE, OSCAR:	For usage of "Wildean", see STOPPARD, TOM.
WORDSWORTH, WILLIAM:	Pastoral. Frequently used in the form "Wordsworthian" to describe the same things as LEE, LAURIE. Also more or less interchangeable with the adjective "Laura Ashley".
WODEHOUSE, P.G.:	Eccentric. Anyone who has been to public school and behaves oddly is described as "like something out of P.G. Wodehouse". Also sometimes used, as well as COWARD, NOËL and FITZGERALD, SCOTT to describe cocktail shakers, etc.

RESPONSES TO

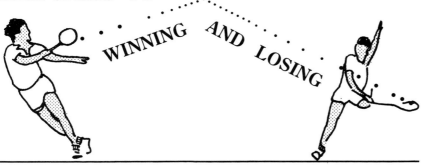

WINNING AND LOSING

People are playing games all the time, and never more so than when they are actually playing games. The aim of most organised sports is TO WIN, to prove oneself SUPERIOR to another member of the species. And the primal instinct of every human being, on winning, is to leap around shouting:

"I BEAT YOU! SEE, I'M BETTER THAN YOUR ARE! NER-NER-NE-NER-NER!"

Equally, the primal instinct of every human being, on being beaten, is to leap around shouting:

"IT WASN'T FAIR! I SHOULD HAVE WON! I'M BETTER THAN YOU! CHEAT!"

However, society tends to disapprove of these unadorned responses (unless they come from international tennis stars, in which case the public feels cheated if it doesn't get them). In Britain that kind of thing is thought to be foreign and unsporting (on a par with training really hard, developing natural talent at a very young age or having adequate sports facilities).

Convention demands that a patina of bonhomie be laid over such feelings, and for the uninitiated it can sometimes be difficult to tell exactly what the participants really mean at the end of a game.

But PEOPLE-SPOTTERS need never be at a loss. The ensuing translations make clear exactly what the players mean. These examples are taken as overheard through the steam in changing-room at a squash club, but could apply equally to tennis, badminton or any other game for two participants.

REMARK

REAL MEANING

"I really enjoyed that." → "I lost, sod it."

"It's a psychological game, isn't it?" → "I lost, sod it."

"It's all about who's in form on the day." → "I lost, sod it."

"So long as I get a bit of exercise, I'm not too worried about the result." → "I lost, sod it."

"I don't think I've ever known a game with so many lets." → "I lost, because you cheated."

(AFTER SWAYING AND PUTTING A HAND TO THE HEAD) "Sorry I've had this 'flu bug. Been in bed all day, but I didn't want to cry off at the last minute." → "I may have lost, but at least I'm going to see that you don't get any satisfaction out of winning."

(AFTER WINCING WITH PAIN) "Ooh! Sorry, I've got this thing with my knee. I didn't mention it, because I thought it'd be O.K., but it flared up in the middle of the first game and…" → "I may have lost, but at least I'm going to see that you don't get any satisfaction out of winning."

(AFTER WINCING WITH PAIN) "Ooh! Sorry, I've got this thing with my knee. I didn't mention it, because I thought it'd be O.K., but it flared up in the middle of the first game and…" → "I've won, and now I'm *really* going to make you feel small."

"You were really playing a storm." → "And I still won - so there!"

"You've really got some amazing shots." → "And I still won - so there!"

"Yes, it is difficult to fit the games in, isn't it?" → "I won, because you're so bloody unfit."

"I had a few lucky bounces, I must say." → "Not only did I beat you at squash, I am also a morally superior person."

"For when the One Great Scorer comes to write against your name, He marks - not that you won or lost - But how you played the game." → "I may have lost, but at least I'm better educated than you are."

"Still, that's the name of the game…" → "I lost, sod it!"

HOLIDAY DIARY

MOST PEOPLE LIE ABOUT THEIR HOLIDAYS. It doesn't do to admit it was a disaster. And that fiction must be maintained in the postcards sent back home, as skilled PEOPLE-SPOTTERS may observe from the following examples:

DIARY OF REAL EVENTS: **DAY 1**

Family arrives at hotel on Greek island, hot and tired after three hours of overexcited children on plane and hour-long hot coach journey on bad road. Children quarrelsome. Tears.

Hotel rooms discovered to be smaller than in brochure, without seaview. Wife says husband ought to complain. Husband says he's far too tired. Recrimination.

Family goes for walk on beach, very aware of the fact that everyone's English; also of the tar, plastic bottles and contemptuous looks from bronzed supermen and superwomen. Husband seems, in wife's view, to be showing excessive interest in toplessness. Recrimination.

Taverna for quiet drink. Child drops lemonade bottle on stone floor and cuts foot on broken glass. Tears.

Evening meal in hotel. Children don't like food. Tears. Husband drinks too much. Recrimination.

Wife says it should be a holiday for her too and husband should put children to bed. He says he's too tired. Recrimination.

Husband and wife go to bed not speaking to each other. Room discovered to be excessively hot. Also directly above hotel disco, just warming up for the night.

Wife speaks to husband enough to say he ought to complain. He says that he's too tired. Recrimination.

Wife sits on balcony shaken by disco music and writes postcard to her mother.

N° .226
KEPKYPA : ΚΑΣΣΙΟΠΗ
CORFU: Kassiopi

Wonderful to be here. Very easy journey. The pace of life is so different. I can just feel all the tensions draining out of me. Hotel idyllic. food lovely. Wine, Sand, Sun— what more could anyone ask? England seems a distant hazy memory. Love from us all.

Mrs. J. P. Grange,
Heathview,
Roundtrees Lane,
Godalming.
Surrey. ENGLAND

Children wake up at six and pound into parents' room. Bawled out by father with crunching hangover. Tears.

Wife tries on bikini and asks husband to give his honest opinion on how she looks. He does. Recrimination.

Family finally makes it to beach, overloaded with baggage, and finds spot apparently not too covered with tar. Wife, daringly revealing one-piece school-style bathing costume, asks husband to anoint exposed flesh with oil. This he does, eyes glued to superbly brown topless hairdresser from Barnsley. Wife notices. Recrimination.

Taverna lunch. Children complain about absence of tomato ketchup and won't eat anything. Tears.

Husband has a go at windsurfing. Spends an hour falling off board. Conscious of contempt of bronzed superman windsurfing instructor.

After silent supper at hotel, children put to bed early. Tears. Husband and wife also to bed early. Husband, thinking of topless hairdresser from Barnsley, touches wife's shoulder. Scream of anguish from sunburn. Recrimination.

Wife goes to sleep.

Husband goes on to balcony with bottle of Greek brandy and writes postcard to lads at the office.

Nº. 226
KEPKYPA: ΚΑΣΣΙΟΠΗ
CORFU: Kassiopi

FOTOTECHNICA ΑΦΟΙ ΚΟΚΚΑΛΗ ΚΕΡΚΥΡΑ-ΤΗΛ. 28-105

Cor – this is the life, eh? Really going native. Sun, sea, booze – wow! Losing all my inhibitions – so's the wife!!! and the windsurfing's terrific! Think I was always cut out to be a beach-bum. Tell old Parsons if I'm not back Friday week I've been seduced by the siren call of the islands! Love to the typing pool.
Paul

ΕΛΛΗΝΙΚΗ ΔΗΜΟΚΡΑΤΙΑ
HELLAS
27

All on the eleventh floor,
J J and D.
Doric Tower
Cheesemarket Lane
London E.C. 1, ENGLAND

© Trimboli – Via Puccini, 67 Pescara (Italia)

DAY 3

Wife woken 3 a.m. by child suffering from diarrhoea. Woken 4.30 by second child suffering from diarrhoea. Husband wakes 6.30 suffering from diahorrea compounded by effects of Greek brandy. Wife gamely tries to make it down to breakfast, but is caught short on the way. Family spends day between bed and lavatory. Greek attitude to toilet paper leads to tears and recrimination.

DAYS 4 - 12

Stomach upsets continue. No food eaten. No sex-life. Brief, uneasy forays made on to beach. As husband gets better, he starts to worry about what's going on in the office. Wife writes some postcards to local friends.

N⁰ .226
KEPKYPA : ΚΑΣΣΙΟΠΗ
CORFU: Kassiopi

Heavenly out here. So peaceful and idyllic. It really makes one question all those materialistic values. Local supermarket is a bit different from Sainsbury's! Kids had a minor tummy bug. but otherwise all blooming! Will need very heavy aerobics after all this wine and food! Lots of love,
Sally.

Wendy Wallace,
17 Claremont Lane,
London SW17.

ENGLAND

© Trimboli - Via Puccini, 67 Pescara (Italia)

DAY 13

Family all fit again. Day spent on beach. Wife observes with disquiet that people who arrived a week later are browner than she is. Risks wearing bikini. Husband makes ill-advised comment on this. Recrimination.

Husband goes for a walk. Falls into conversation with topless hairdresser from Barnsley. Returns to wife. Recrimination.

Husband sits on sand, watching bronzed superman windsurfing instructor pirouetting over the water. Feels bored. Can't wait to get back to the office.

All go to taverna party in evening. Children don't like food. Tears.

Husband does Greek dancing with hairdresser from Barnsley.

In bed tries yet again, only to have behaviour with hairdresser from Barnsley thrown in his face. Recrimination. Wife goes to sleep.

Husband goes out on to balcony shaken by disco music with what's left of bottle of Greek brandy. Sees hairdresser from Barnsley going down on to beach with bronzed superman windsurfing instructor and lascivious intent. Writes postcard to boss.

N°.226
ΚΕΡΚΥΡΑ: ΚΑΣΣΙΟΠΗ
CORFU: Kassiopi

Dear Mr. Parsons,

Having a really terrific time out here, lotus-eating. Lovely to have some time with the wife and kids. Sorry to say I haven't thought about the office once. Still, what are holidays for? Hope all is well with you. Friday week I'll be the bronzed one in the corner!

Yours sincerely,
Paul Blacksee

FOTOTECHNICA ΑΦΟΙ ΚΟΚΚΑΛΗ ΚΕΡΚΥΡΑ - ΤΗΛ. 28-105

HELLAS

ΕΛΛΗΝΙΚΗ ΔΗΜΟΚΡΑΤΙΑ 27

H.P.R.D.,
J.J. and D.,
Doric Tower,
Cheesemarket Lane,
London, E.C.1, ENGLAND

© Trimboli – Via Puccini, 67 Pescara (Italia)

Day spent on beach. All very relaxed. Wife takes off bikini top and hides behind dune for half an hour.

At evening meal in hotel, husband observes to children that they'll be home within twenty-four hours. Tears.

Hotel proprietor, in expansive mood, offers ouzo. Husband, who has been drinking Greek brandy, agrees. Wife goes up to put children to bed.

Husband eventually totters up to join her. Wife says she'll be with him in a minute, giving him a meaningful kiss as she disappears into shower-room. Husband, thinking of topless hairdresser from Barnsley, takes all his clothes off and gets into bed. Wife emerges from shower-room to find husband
snoring loudly. Wife goes out on to balcony
shaken by disco music and writes
postcard to old schoolfriend.

Early start, vertiginous coach-ride and crowded aeroplane do little for husband's hangover. Tears and recrimination.

Family arrives home late afternoon and starts queuing up for the phone to tell friends what a wonderful holiday they've had.

N°.226
ΚΕΡΚΥΡΑ : ΚΑΣΣΙΟΠΗ
CORFU: Kassiopi

Wonderfully relaxing out here, lolling on the beach all day in just a bikini bottom. Great social life, too and in spite of the kids, a bit of a second honeymoon! Only cloud on the horizon is the thought of having to come back! Really makes us question the old materialistic values. Even talk about chucking it all and moving out here permanently.
love Sally.

Mrs. Laura Green,
Beston Farmhouse,
Ramsbury, Wilts.

ENGLAND.

FOTOTECHNICA ΑΦΙΟΙ ΚΟΚΚΑΛΗ ΚΕΡΚΥΡΑ

HELLAS

ΕΛΛΗΝΙΚΗ ΔΗΜΟΚΡΑΤΙΑ 27

H-EXPR

© Trimboli - Via Puccini, 67 Pescara (Italia)

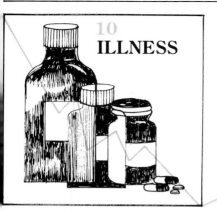

10 ILLNESS

There are two sorts of illness - 1., SUFFERED ILLNESS (the sort the sufferer talks to the doctor about and other people talk about behind the sufferer's back), and, 2., DISCUSSED ILLNESS (the sort the sufferer himself or herself talks about to people other than the doctor). The first sort are physical illnesses over which the sufferer has little control. The second sort may incidentally be physical illnesses, but the sufferer is using them and talking about them with an INTENTION. That INTENTION is that the listener should think one of the following:

1. Poor thing.
2. It's not really fair to judge someone with a disability like that by normal standards.
3. Isn't it remarkable how he/she manages to achieve so much in spite of that kind of disability?

However, as is so often the case, the INTENTION rarely gets the response it aims for. On hearing someone talking about an illness, the most common REACTIONS from the listener are the following:

1. I'm not interested in your aches and pains.
2. I've got it worse than you have and I'm not making a fuss.
3. Thank you. That's just the cue I need to start talking about my illness.

Certain specific ailments prompt specific REACTIONS. The following lines:

"It's my back"
"It's my tummy.", or
"It's the usual/same old trouble."

will always elicit in the listener the same unspoken response:
IT'S PSYCHOSOMATIC.

The statement:

"I'VE GOT A COLD",

issued with the INTENTION of achieving a "POOR THING" response, unfailingly achieves the following two REACTIONS:

1. So what?
2. Then don't come near me, you selfish bastard.

The following list of DISCUSSED ILLNESSES, all talked about with the INTENTION of provoking at least one of the three basic responses outlined about (*POOR THING,* etc), in fact always get the REACTION detailed below:

STATEMENT	REACTION
"I've got a touch of 'flu."	)
"I've got a bit of a throat."	)**All right, so you've got**
"The old sinuses are playing up."	)**a cold.** (Followed by
"I've got a streptococcic infection."	)cold reactions detailed
"I've got a bit of a temperature."	)above.)
"I think I may have picked up some sort of virus."	)
"I've got bronchitis."	)
"I've got piles."	)
"I've got hives."	)**Tee-hee!***
"I've got shingles."	)

* (This is a most unfair reaction, because all three illnesses are extremely painful. However, possibly because of their silly names, that is how people do react to them, so the sufferer would be well-advised to keep quiet about the subject.)

STATEMENT	REACTION
"I've got a migraine."	All right, so you've got a headache.
"I've got a touch of malaria."	All right, I know you're just showing off about all the places you've been.
"I've got a touch of V.D."	(As above)
"I must tell you about my operation."	Oh, Jesus, no! Anything but that. Dear, oh dear, is that the time? I've just remembered I have a very pressing engagement. Goodbye.

As a basic rule, listeners are always particularly sceptical of sufferers who are possessive about their illnesses. Speaking of something as "my" illness implies a degree of love for it, and also seems to demand a continuing indulgence for the condition which the listener may well not be willing to grant. People are doubly resistant to any DISCUSSED ILLNESS statement which begins:
"I've got one of my..."
and continues:
"backs/tummies/colds/throats/headaches/migraines...",etc.

Rather in the way that they reject the idea of owning a British car as being too boring, many Middle Class people express a preference for alternative medicine (unless of course they're really ill, in which case they'll swallow any chemical traditional medicine prescribes).

The chief reason for this is that it sounds more interesting. Comments about DISCUSSED ILLNESSES which begin:

"My doctor thinks that it's..."

sound pretty dull, and elitist variants of this, like:

"My consultant seems pretty sure that it's..."

"My specialist has a nasty feeling it may be..." or even:

"My surgeon is afraid he may have to..."

are now too commonplace to have much impact.

How much more effective are lines which begin:

"My osteopath has a feeling in his bones that..."

"My acupuncturist has put his finger on it..."

"My homeopathist's opinion is...", or

"My hypnotherapist reckons..."

The trouble is that, like all forms of Oneupmanship, this suffers from the Law of Diminishing Returns. When everyone's talking about their acupuncturist, the word no longer has the power to impress. As a result, people are driven to ever more obscure forms of alternative medicine, and now it is not uncommon to hear such attention-grabbing lines as the following:

"My naturopathist is convinced that...",

"My aromatherapist has no doubt at all that..", or

"In my reflexologist's view..."

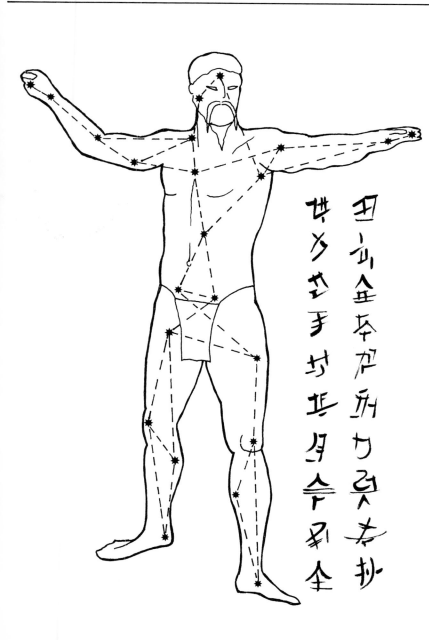

Of course, there is no end to this escalation of obscurity, and PEOPLE-SPOTTERS are advised that the only possible way of keeping their end up in such conversations is to refer to a system of alternative medicine even more obscure than any the people they're talking to can come up with.

As a bonus to buyers of this book, here is a body chart for the ancient Chinese healing art of Seng Ding, or anointing with honey. The dots on the body show the main anointing points, while the list down the side enumerates the afflictions cured by anointing on the respective points.

SEXUAL BRAGGING

Men are expected to brag about their sexual exploits – or at least men seem to think they're expected to brag about their sexual exploits. Certainly, if they didn't, there would be long silences in many offices, and publicans would have to keep turning up the muzak to fill in the pauses. Needless to say, sexual bragging is not always completely truthful, and PEOPLE-SPOTTERS should consult the following list to find out the real meaning of certain commonly-heard remarks:

REMARK	REAL MEANING
"If I don't get it once a day, I start to feel twitchy."	"If I don't say this once a day, I start to feel twitchy."
"I mean, I don't see myself as a stud or anything, but…"	"I do see myself as a stud."
"I'd never thought of myself as anything out of the ordinary."	"I've always thought of myself as something out of the ordinary."
"I've always liked women."	"I've always lusted after women."
"I can't help it."	"I make no attempt to help it."
"I can't remember how many women I've had."	"I can remember exactly how many women I've had, but I'm not going to tell you, in case you've had more."
"I don't know, last night it must have been…four…five times?"	"I do know. Last night it was twice."
"God, when I think back to all the girls I had before I got married."	"There were two or three — honestly."
"I've never had any complaints."	"My wife thinks I'm good."
"Impotence has never been one of my worries."	"Impotence has always been one of my worries."
"Well, I suppose I am quite highly sexed."	"I want sex marginally more often than she does."
"She's a nymphomaniac."	"She wants sex marginally more often than I do."
"She's frigid."	"I wasn't very good."

"She was insatiable."

"Let's just say it was good —
no need to go into the details."

"…but then a gentleman doesn't
mention the lady's name."

"Wow, she was panting for it."

"I thought I knew it all, but she
really taught me a thing or two."

"I'd always thought she was the
quiet type, but, wow, in bed…"

"God, I had to fight her off. It
was all there, if I'd fancied it."

"….but I'm a normal red-
blooded man, for God's sake."

"…and so long as no one gets
hurt, where's the harm."

"It was just pure sexual
chemistry."

"… and, let's face it, sexual
guilt went out in the Fifties."

"… and rather than the urge
getting less as I get older."

"…you know what I mean…?"

"…need I say more…?

"I came too quickly."

"I am about to tell you all the
details."

"I am about to tell you the lady's
name."

"She responded exactly as I had
hoped she would, and now I feel
slight distaste."

"I am quite innocent really."

"She scared me witless."

"She wouldn't let me."

"I feel guilty about having
cheated on my wife."

"I feel guilty about having
cheated on my wife."

"I feel guilty about having
cheated on my wife."

"I feel guilty about having
cheated on my wife."

"I can still just do it, thank
God."

"Whether you do or not, I'm still
going to tell you — at great
length.

"There is nothing more to say."

SEX

Everyone suffers from prurient interest in sex. One of the wonderful things about books like this one is that it enables people to indulge that prurient interest under the guise of scientific enquiry.

Below are a series of graphs purporting to analyse sexual behaviour. In each case the unbroken line indicates the male response and the broken line the female response. Time is represented along the horizontal line and level of sexual arousal up the vertical line. Arousal is measured in ergs. (This unit is used because it approximates most closely to the noises uttered during sexual activity.) As will be seen, arousal is measured from the peak of MAJOR ORGASM down to the bottom line of SLEEP. Other variations of measurement are indicated in individual graphs.

*N.B. For men under 18, these times should be read as seconds; for men over 50, as hours. Men over 70 might be well advised to think in terms of weeks (or maybe just forget it).

TEXTBOOK INTERCOURSE

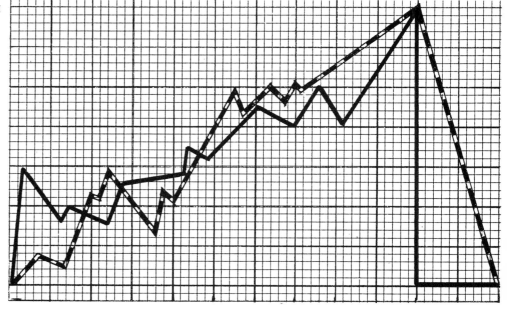

EROTIC AROUSAL LEVEL IN ERGS

MAJOR ORGASM

MINOR ORGASM

MINI ORGASM

SLEEP LINE

TIME IN MINUTES*

5 10 15 20 25 30 35 40 45 50 55 60

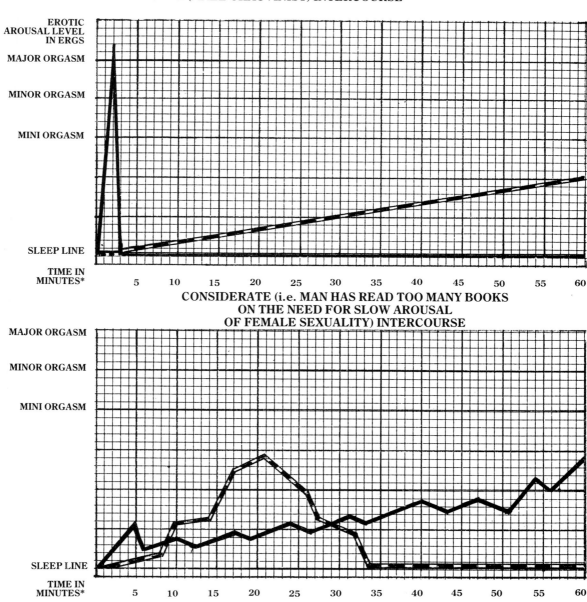

TRADITIONAL (MALE CHAUVINIST) INTERCOURSE

EROTIC AROUSAL LEVEL IN ERGS

MAJOR ORGASM

MINOR ORGASM

MINI ORGASM

SLEEP LINE

TIME IN MINUTES*

5 10 15 20 25 30 35 40 45 50 55 60

CONSIDERATE (i.e. MAN HAS READ TOO MANY BOOKS ON THE NEED FOR SLOW AROUSAL OF FEMALE SEXUALITY) INTERCOURSE

MAJOR ORGASM

MINOR ORGASM

MINI ORGASM

SLEEP LINE

TIME IN MINUTES*

5 10 15 20 25 30 35 40 45 50 55 60

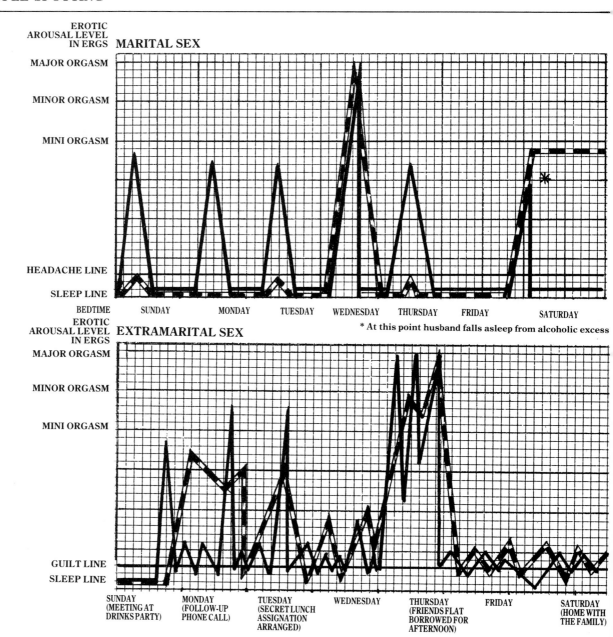

MARITAL SEX

EROTIC
AROUSAL LEVEL
IN ERGS

MAJOR ORGASM

MINOR ORGASM

MINI ORGASM

HEADACHE LINE

SLEEP LINE

BEDTIME   SUNDAY   MONDAY   TUESDAY   WEDNESDAY   THURSDAY   FRIDAY   SATURDAY

* At this point husband falls asleep from alcoholic excess

EXTRAMARITAL SEX

EROTIC
AROUSAL LEVEL
IN ERGS

MAJOR ORGASM

MINOR ORGASM

MINI ORGASM

GUILT LINE

SLEEP LINE

SUNDAY
(MEETING AT
DRINKS PARTY)

MONDAY
(FOLLOW-UP
PHONE CALL)

TUESDAY
(SECRET LUNCH
ASSIGNATION
ARRANGED)

WEDNESDAY

THURSDAY
(FRIENDS FLAT
BORROWED FOR
AFTERNOON)

FRIDAY

SATURDAY
(HOME WITH
THE FAMILY)

11
SPIRITUAL LIFE

Church-going used to be one of the major manifestations of Middle Class behaviour, but times have changed. Now rather less people in the country regularly attend church than listen to Radio Four (and indeed many seem to believe that Radio Four has taken over the role of moral arbiter once occupied by the Church of England). However, this change in Sunday habits does not mean that the Middle Class is devoid of spiritual life. It is simply that the emphasis of that spiritual life has shifted away from the more conventional outlets.

Indeed, because one of the most significant Middle Class characteristics is **Guilt**, a great many non-church-goers still feel guilty about the fact that they don't attend, and get a mild *frisson* of wickedness from such activities as cinema-going on a Sunday.

And there are those who still go to church, finding in the simple Christian activities of dominating committees, arranging flowers better than the person who did it last week, or bitching about the vicar, opportunities for the expression of that other Middle Class characteristic, **Aspiration**.

Others approach religion rather as they do medicine. In the same way that people draw attention to themselves by ignoring the N.H.S. and resorting to alternative therapies, so many discard the Anglican Church in favour of more unusual creeds. How much more interesting than admitting at a dinner party to being "boring old C of E", runs the theory, to claim to be a Confucian, Shintoist or Zoroastrian. (This is actually based on a fallacy. Nothing quietens a dinner party quicker than talk of religion. And, if someone really wants to empty the room in a hurry, they should claim to be a "born-again Christian".)

Another popular way of drawing attention to oneself through one's spiritual identity is by resorting to those vague areas of superstition like Tarot cards and astrology. The latter, of course, has probably provided more corny opening lines in conversation than any other subject in the last twenty years. Later in this section will be found a PEOPLE-SPOTTER'S guide to the "Signs of the Zodiac".

But first, overleaf, is a means of assessing people's attitude to more conventional religion.

RELIGIOMETER

An at-a-glance aid for PEOPLE-SPOTTERS which will enable them to know instantly from people's pronouncements on the subject exactly how religious they are.

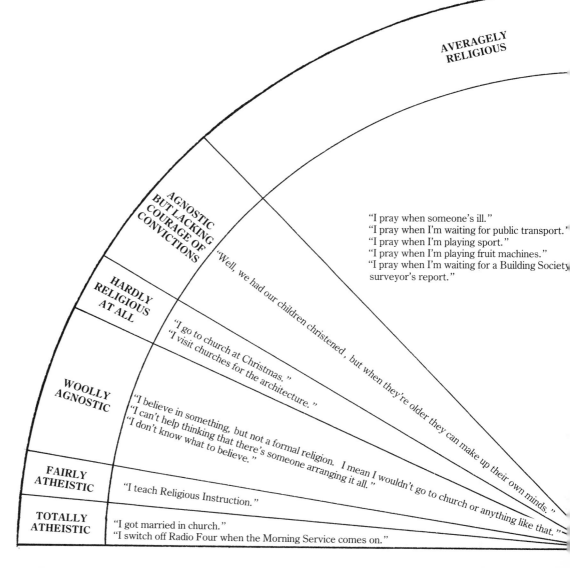

AVERAGELY RELIGIOUS

AGNOSTIC BUT LACKING COURAGE OF CONVICTIONS

HARDLY RELIGIOUS AT ALL

WOOLLY AGNOSTIC

FAIRLY ATHEISTIC

TOTALLY ATHEISTIC

"I pray when someone's ill."
"I pray when I'm waiting for public transport."
"I pray when I'm playing sport."
"I pray when I'm playing fruit machines."
"I pray when I'm waiting for a Building Society surveyor's report."

"Well, we had our children christened, but when they're older they can make up their own minds."

"I go to church at Christmas."
"I visit churches for the architecture."

"I believe in something, but not a formal religion. I mean I wouldn't go to church or anything like that."

"I can't help thinking that there's someone arranging it all."
"I don't know what to believe."

"I teach Religious Instruction."

"I got married in church."
"I switch off Radio Four when the Morning Service comes on."

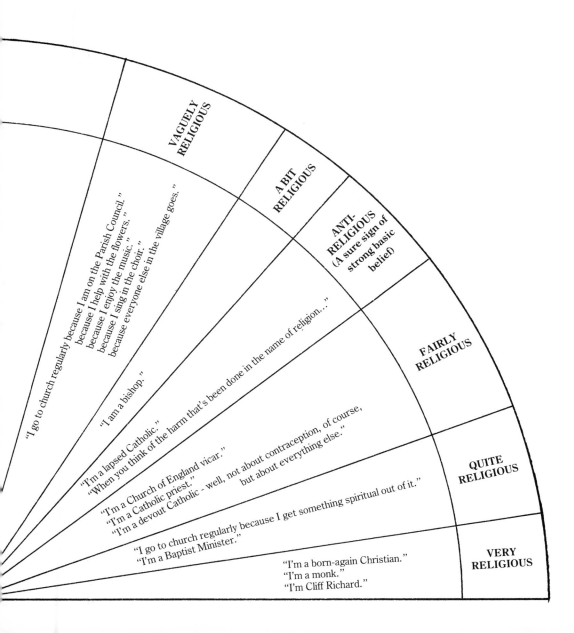

VAGUELY RELIGIOUS

A BIT RELIGIOUS

ANTI-RELIGIOUS
(A sure sign of strong basic belief)

FAIRLY RELIGIOUS

QUITE RELIGIOUS

VERY RELIGIOUS

"I go to church regularly because I am on the Parish Council."
because I help with the flowers."
because I enjoy the music."
because I sing in the choir."
because everyone else in the village goes."

"I am a bishop."

"I'm a lapsed Catholic."

"When you think of the harm that's been done in the name of religion..."

"I'm a Church of England vicar."
"I'm a Catholic priest."
"I'm a devout Catholic - well, not about contraception, of course, but about everything else."

"I go to church regularly because I get something spiritual out of it."
"I'm a Baptist Minister."

"I'm a born-again Christian."
"I'm a monk."
"I'm Cliff Richard."

ASTROLOGY

Astrology is one of the most appealing of the pseudosciences, because there is something in it for everyone. Whatever the predictions in the newspaper say, every reader can find some personal pertinence in them. Astrology offers the supreme ego-massage. Everyone has a sign supposed to represent certain personality traits, and they can be delightfully selective in which ones they apply to themselves. At the same time they can be delightfully dismissive of people born under other signs. Specially for PEOPLE-SPOTTERS, here are the details of the characteristics attributed to the twelve Signs of the Zodiac, first, by those born under each sign, and, second, by those not born under the sign:

SIGN	CHARACTERISTICS AS SEEN BY SOMEBODY BORN UNDER THE SAME SIGN	CHARACTERISTICS AS SEEN BY SOMEBODY BORN UNDER ANOTHER SIGN
ARIES (21 March - 20 April)	Energetic Enthusiastic Courageous Optimistic	Reckless Inconsiderate Wilful Egotistical
TAURUS (21 April - 20 May)	Impeturbable Well-organised Resolute Good with money	Dull Nit-picking Stubborn Mean
GEMINI (21 May - 20 June)	Generous Outgoing Quick-witted Artistic	Extravagant Hearty Capricious Pretentious

SIGN	CHARACTERISTICS AS SEEN BY SOMEBODY BORN UNDER THE SAME SIGN	CHARACTERISTICS AS SEEN BY SOMEBODY BORN UNDER ANOTHER SIGN

* *

CANCER
(21 June -
21 July)

Sympathetic	Nosey
Patient	Procrastinating
Self-reliant	Self-centred
Serene	Smug

*   *   *

LEO
(22 July -
21 August)

Dignified	Pompous
Commanding	Bossy
Prudent	Pussy-footed
Tolerant	Lazy

*   *   *

VIRGO
(22 August -
22 September)

Discriminating	Fussy
Shrewd	Calculating
Hard-working	Officious
Accurate	Too clever by half

SIGN	CHARACTERISTICS AS SEEN BY SOMEBODY BORN UNDER THE SAME SIGN	CHARACTERISTICS AS SEEN BY SOMEBODY BORN UNDER ANOTHER SIGN

* *

LIBRA (23 September - 22 October	Balanced Adaptable Kindly Tactful	Characterless Indecisive Sentimental Wishy-washy

*   *   *

SCORPIO (23 October - 22 November)	Thorough Purposeful Vigilant Ingenious	Infuriating Inconsiderate Suspicious Devious

*   *   *

SAGITTARIUS (23 November - 20 December)	Honest Independent Sporty Decisive	Rude Bloody-minded Bumptious Self-opinionated

SIGN	CHARACTERISTICS AS SEEN BY SOMEBODY BORN UNDER THE SAME SIGN	CHARACTERISTICS AS SEEN BY SOMEBODY BORN UNDER ANOTHER SIGN

* *

CAPRICORN
(21 December -
19 January)

Enterprising
Dedicated
Diplomatic
Disciplined

Go-getting
Bigoted
Unscrupulous
Insensitive

✻ ✻ ✻

AQUARIUS
(20 January -
18 February)

Calm
Sincere
Reasonable
Spiritual

Apathetic
Boring
Insipid
Impractical

✻ ✻ ✻

PISCES
(19 February -
20 March)

Idealistic
Romantic
Imaginative
Warm

Clueless
Clinging
Day-dreaming
Soppy

THE MIDDLE CLASS PRAYER

Our Father, which art in Heaven *(or at least the possibility of whose being in Heaven makes it a reasonable precaution to pray to You).*
Hallowed be Thy name *(well, not so much hallowed as used, particularly when shouting at the kids, banging thumbs with hammers, and responding to news of friends' divorces or the rising price of mangetouts).*
Thy kingdom come *(in the sense that we strongly support the idea of equality and plenty for everyone in the world, so long as achieving that goal does not in any way diminish our standard of living).*
Thy will be done in earth, as it is in Heaven *(that is, of course, so long as Thy will doesn't conflict too much with our will).*
Give us this day our daily bread *(wholemeal, of course – not to mention our daily unsalted butter, free-range eggs, organically grown vegetables, Marks & Spencers quiches, gin and tonics...oh, and the odd bottle of Sainsbury's plonk).*
And forgive us our trespasses *(well, except of course for adultery, which, let's face it, is really so much part of modern life and frequently important both to strengthen one's marriage and to help one develop as a personality),* as we forgive those who trespass against us *(except of course for people who commit the cardinal sin of Doing Better than us).*
And lead us not into temptation *(except, of course, for adultery – see above),* but deliver us from evil *(particularly the evil of redundancy).*
For thine is the kingdom, the power, and the glory *(well, except for our house, family and possessions, which are, after all, the fullest expression of us rather than of You).*
For ever and ever *(or at least until the kids have finished school and we've paid off the mortgage).*

Amen

CONVERSATION 12

Like so many of its other activities, conversation for the Middle Class is a competitive exercise. Its dominant motivation of insecurity ensures that the species always enters a conversational exchange in the hope of emerging victorious. Victory is assessed according to a complex system of points. There are many different ways in which these points can be gained. Sometimes conversations follow the scoring systems of games. A **Tennis Conversation**, for instance, is won by the first participant to score four points (though there is often a lot of manoeuvring for advantage round "Deuce").

In a **Squash Conversation**, a point can only be scored by someone who has already gained the initiative, so the game alternates between sudden rushes of points and long to-and-fro exchanges in which nobody scores. (This is the basic format of most marital conversations.)

Then of course there is the **Cricket Conversation**, in which the aim is to bore one's opponent into submission.

But whether the talk follows a formalised pattern or not, point-scoring remains the sole aim. Any conversational claim made by the opponent must be countered, topped or diminished.

The methods of achieving these ends vary a great deal, but generally subtlety is appreciated. Blatant boasting or actually shouting down one's opponent (also known as **Football Conversation**) would commit the unforgivable Middle Class sin of being *"common"*. The ideal is always to observe the niceties of politeness, and to keep a genteel smile screwed firmly in position as the blows are delivered.

There are many conversational weapons in the Middle Class armoury. Obscure references, casually dropped names, foreign words... all these can be deployed to cause maximum discomfiture.

But this can be most easily achieved by the straight Counter-Response, a put-down (frequently in the form of a question) which, when properly used, is guaranteed to leave the opponent with egg on the face, a subdued "Oh" dying on the lips.

Since this conversational weapon is so prevalent, it is important that PEOPLE-SPOTTERS should be able to recognise when a Middle Class Counter-Response is being used, and, to that end, there follow a few examples, applying to the areas of Possessions, Travel, Children's Achievements, and Wine.

COUNTER-RESPONSES IN CONVERSATIONS ABOUT POSSESSIONS

"We've just got this microcomputer."
"Oh yes, I remember those."

"Do have a look at this. Apparently there were very few of them made."
"One can see why."

"The man in the shop swore it was genuine."
"They do have a nerve, these people, don't they?"

"It's real silk/silver/mahogany, etc."
"Is there another sort?"

"It once belonged to (famous name).*"*
"Oh yes, notorious old jackdaw, wasn't he?"

"We're absolutely crazy about this porcelain."
"You'd have to be, wouldn't you?"

"Have you seen this painting? It's an original."
"Yes, well, one can hardly imagine anyone reproducing it, can one?"

COUNTER-RESPONSES IN CONVERSATION ABOUT TRAVEL

"The flight wasn't too bad - a bit of waiting around, of course - you know, you have to check in two hours before."
"Good heavens, have I finally met someone who actually does that?"

"Oh no, it was a scheduled flight."
"Next thing you'll be telling me you actually paid the full fare."

"I travel light - everything in the one suitcase."
"You take a suitcase, do you?"

"It's a tiny village, way off the beaten track, completely primitive, really."
"Oh yes, we used to go there before it got spoilt."

"We go there every year and we're treated just like the locals."
"I thought all the locals had moved away."

"Of course, there's only one hotel to stay at there."
"Yes, the Paradiso (or any other obscure name that's going to nonplus the opposition)."

"The proprietor really made us feel part of the family."
"Hypocritical old bugger, isn't he?"

"I don't know if you know New York/Tokyo/Bangkok etc. at all...?"
"Well, I haven't been there for a couple of months."

COUNTER-RESPONSES IN CONVERSATIONS ABOUT CHILDREN'S ACHIEVEMENT

"There's a lot of his father in him."
"Oh, I'm sure he'll learn to cope with that in time."

"He's crawling now."
"With what?"

"He's got the family brains/looks."
"Well, somebody must have, mustn't they?"

"He's a little terror, isn't he?"
"Yes."

"The teachers say it's a really quite exceptional talent."
"Must be hell having one of those jobs where you always have to say the right thing, mustn't it?"

"What do you think of this picture he's done? Go on, be honest."
"Ah, now that wouldn't be fair, would it?"

"He's been selected to play for the school."
"I think it's wonderful the way they give everyone a chance, don't you?"

"He thinks he can charm his way out of anything."
"Well, I'm sure someone will soon put him right on that."

COUNTER-RESPONSES IN CONVERSATION ABOUT WINE

"I don't hold with all this wine snobbery. So long as I'm drinking something that's reasonably priced and alcoholic, that's all that matters to me."
"Evidently."

"We just have this wine for quaffing."
"Well, you wouldn't want to do anything else with it, would you?"

"What's more, it's dirt cheap."
"That figures."

"Actually, it's methode champenoise, *but I find I can hardly tell the difference."*
"Really?"

"A few weeks ago I tried some of the '82."
"Oh, bad luck."

"I hope the Muscadet's cold enough."
"It's cold enough to go with the steak, certainly."

"Now I don't want to tell you what it is, so I'm going to hide the label."
"Very wise."

"I don't know if you've tried this Moroccan Burgundy...?"
"Well, yes, of course I have. In Morocco."

FOREIGN WORDS

Language is continually on the move, and English has always assimilated words from other countries. These borrowed words are used to give tone to the speaker's conversation, but their meaning is frequently inexact. Here is a list of foreign words and phrases, together with their meanings as currently used by the PEOPLE-SPOTTER'S quarry, the Middle Class.

AD HOC: An adjective used to describe a party which has been planned for ages, but for which the invitations have only been issued at the last minute. "Do come round if you can. It's all going to be very AD HOC."

À LA CARTE: Expensive. Used only in the sentence, "There's a set menu, unless of course you'd rather go A LA CARTE...?" (The perfect example of that Latin construction, A Question Expecting The Answer "No".)

AMBIENCE: Whether a restaurant has piped music or not. A restaurant without piped music is said to have "a good AMBIENCE"; a restaurant with piped music is said to have "something wrong with the AMBIENCE."

ANGST: Mild discussion, as in, "We couldn't decide whether to go to Corfu or the Algarve this year. We went through a lot of ANGST about it."

AU PAIR: An anorexic or promiscuous foreign girl employed by people with more money than the speaker.

AVANT GARDE: Used as an adjective to describe any artistic experience the speaker did not understand.

BONA FIDES: Cheque guarantee card, as in the sentence, "The stupid girl behind the counter wouldn't accept it until I had established my BONA FIDES."

BON VIVEUR: A fat man with an expense account.

BOURGEOIS: Every member of the Middle Class except the person speaking.

CARBONNADE: Any sort of stew.

CREDO: An opinion. "It's always been part of my CREDO that Brie should be really runny."

CRÈME DE LA CRÈME: A secretary who doesn't have to make the coffee.

CURRICULUM VITAE: A work of fiction whose compostion fills the time of the newly-redundant.

ENFANT TERRIBLE: A description, only used retrospectively, of someone who has become a pillar of the establishment. "He used to be a bit of an ENFANT TERRIBLE."

EX GRATIA:	Tax-free.
HAUSFRAU:	A disparaging term used to describe a woman who runs her house more efficiently than the speaker.
IMPASSE:	The stage of a marriage when neither partner can raise a subject without starting an argument. "I'm afraid Neville and Sue have reached an absolute IMPASSE."
LOCUM:	A different doctor who does not appreciate the seriousness of the speaker's condition.
MAGNUM OPUS:	A novel which does not get finished.
NOUVEAU RICHE:	Anyone with more money than the speaker.
PIÈCE DE RESISTANCE:	A recent purchase, sometimes a garment, but more often a large kitchen appliance, like a fridge-freezer. "Ah, but you haven't seen the PIÈCE DE RESISTANCE!"
POSEUR:	Someone very similar to the speaker, whom the speaker dislikes. "He's a terrible POSEUR."
SAVOIR FAIRE:	An American Express Gold Card. As in, "He's got SAVOIR FAIRE."
STATUS QUO:	An unsatisfactory situation. "Then he decided he didn't love her, so she's back to the STATUS QUO."
TOUR DE FORCE:	Something that goes on too long. "Then he has this amazing monologue in the Second Act that's a real TOUR DE FORCE."
VERBATIM:	In reporting a conversation, this word is used like the English word "literally", to mean "very approximately".

NAME-DROPPING

Name-dropping has always been one of the most popular human vanities, and PEOPLE-SPOTTERS should be able to recognise when it's being indulged. The following notes on the most common "drops" may prove useful:

THE BLATANT DROP

This one is a bit unsubtle, but is still quite commonly heard in Middle Class circles. It takes the following simple form:

A: You'll never guess who I met last week – Michael Searle-Parker!

Unfortunately, such a remark is in danger of offending the first canon of Middle Class behaviour and sounding *common*. Indeed, that is probably exactly what a member of the Working Class might say, having encountered a member of the cast of, say, *Coronation Street*. To avoid any confusion therefore, though the same formula of words is used in Middle Class circles, it is always delivered in an assumed accent. This accent is either

a) that of a small child,

or   b) that of a *common* person of the sort described above.

Using the accent achieves two things:
1. It ensures that no one misses the actual dropping of the name.
2. At the same time it distances the speaker from the "drop", showing him or her to be a person of discrimination, above being impressed by mere celebrity.

THE COMPLICIT DROP

This one is considerably subtler and, as its name suggests, assumes complicity between the speaker and the person to whom he is speaking. A common form of the COMPLICIT DROP goes like this:

A: I was having dinner last week with old Michael Searle-Parker, who, as I don't need to tell you, can be a bit of a rogue, and he was saying...

This achieves three things:
1. It demonstrates the speaker's easy familiarity with the celebrity in question.
2. By including the person addressed in the acquaintance, it shows the speaker to be above being impressed by mere celebrity.
3. By wrongly assuming that the person addressed knows the celebrity mentioned (and anyone using this "drop" will be extremely careful not to use it to someone who might know him), it makes the person addressed feel small both for the poverty of his own social life and for the shameful fact that he is impressed.

THE IGNORANT DROP

The details may vary, but the most common form of the IGNORANT DROP goes like this:

A: I sat next to a bloke at dinner last week...now what was his name? Apparently I should have heard of him. Michael...something double-barrelled? Searle, I think. Searle-... I don't know, Barker was it?
B: Not Michael Searle-Parker?
A: Yes, I think that was it. Anyway, he was saying...

The important thing to realise about this one is that the speaker is not ignorant at all. If he were genuinely unaware of his subject's celebrity, he would not bother to use the name; he would just say, "A bloke I met at dinner last week was saying..." However, by using the IGNORANT DROP, the speaker has achieved three things:
1. He has established that he moves in rarified social circles where he might meet people like the celebrity mentioned.
2. He has established by his apparent ignorance that he is above being impressed by contact with such celebrities.
3. He has shown up the person he's talking to by making that person actually do the name-dropping for him.

THE RIPOSTE DROP

This is another subtle one, and is used to counter a primary "drop". The form it takes is something like this:

A: At a dinner last week I was sitting next to Michael Searle-Parker and he was saying –
B: Michael, eh ? how's Deirdre ?

B, of course, is calling the shots in this one. His reference to Deirdre should achieve two important things:
1. It will catch A off his guard. A, having just made his "drop", will be in confident mood, expecting an impressed reaction from B, and certainly not expecting to have the wind taken out of his sails by the introduction of Deirdre.

2. It will also, of course, imply B's much greater intimacy with the celebrity than anything that A could hope to achieve. (Before using the ploy, B is going to make sure that A doesn't know the celebrity well. Then he can be confident that there won't be any follow-up questions. A is never going to expose himself further by asking whether Deirdre is the celebrity's wife, or girlfriend, or mother. As a result, B will always be quite safe to make up any name he chooses for the RIPOSTE DROP.)

THE COMPETITIVE DROP

This is a very common form of name-dropping encounter, usually heard in media circles. A famous name is mentioned and the participants then vie with each other to assert the greater intimacy of their own acquaintance with the name dropped.

A: Tell you who I met at a dinner party the other night. Michael Searle-Parker.
B: Oh, really? I haven't seen Michael for yonks. How is the old devil?
A: In pretty good nick, I'd say. Certainly behaved as if he was …but then you know what Mike's like.
B: And how ! Life and soul of every party, that's Mickey.
A: Yes, great mixer, old Mickey-Wicky.
B: Well, I don't know. Fancy you meeting old Searlibobs. Didn't mention me by any chance, did he ?
A: No, your name didn't pass old Parkyboy's lips.
B: No, of course not. That's Fluffy all over, though…
A: Yes, Frou-frou's always been a bit like that, hasn't she ?… etc., etc.,etc…

PEOPLE-SPOTTERS should be warned that this one can go on for ever-and frequently does.

TENSES

Members of the Middle Class pride themselves on their grammar, and watch out beadily for shortcomings in the grammar of others. A split infinitive is pounced on with almost as much glee as a dropped aitch; it is an indication of the speaker's inferiority. But there are distinctive Middle Class usages, particularly of tenses, which should be drawn to the PEOPLE-SPOTTER'S attention.

THE PERMANENT PRESENT

This tense is used very frequently, usually in conjunction with the word always, as in the example:
"We always go to Corfu."
What this usually means is:
"This will be the second year we've gone to Corfu."

THE PAST PERFECT

Another tense that is in common currency, this can usually be recognised by the slight shake of the head and expression of wistfulness with which it is spoken. Examples would include such remarks as:
"Life was just so uninhibited in the Sixties."
"In those days at least the songs had tunes."
"Mind you, that was before we had children."

THE PRESENT IMPERFECT

This one is also sometimes accompanied by a shake of the head or, more commonly, a shrug of helplessness. It is used in constructions like the following:
"I don't know what things are coming to."
"Young people today just don't seem to have any joy in anything they do."
"And the new doctor can hardly speak English."

THE FUTURE IMPERFECT

Used very much in the same way as the above, for example in:
"I don't know where it's all going to end."
"I'm glad I won't be around to see it."
or any sentence beginning, **"And at this rate the world's natural resources..."**

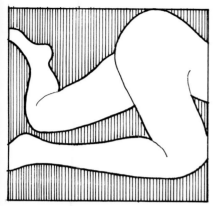

BODY LANGUAGE AND MOVEMENT PATTERNS
13

It is a cliché of pop-anthropology and pop-psychology books that the human body gives out quite as much information as the human voice. Gestures, postures and movements have all been analysed with great academic seriousness, facility and glibness, but to date all these analyses have been generalised. No one has yet investigated the special area of Middle Class Body Language. How privileged then are PEOPLE-SPOTTERS to have available to them the information in the following pages (information, it incidentally might be worth stressing, which is based on research quite as detailed and exhaustive as that which has gone into the rest of this book). Certain postures and gestures, of course, go with certain forms of occupation. The pessimistically jutting lower lip obviously identifies the Servicer announcing his inability to repair your defective appliance and demanding whether you've been having a go at it yourself. The complacently shaken head is characteristic of an Obstructor denying you access to a public building or saying you can't have egg and chips without the beans because the menu says egg and chips *with* beans. The disarming shrug and cheery smile marks out the Fixer asking for more money.

But as well as these occupational body movements, there are others which apply to specifically Middle Class situations, and it is important that a qualified PEOPLE-SPOTTER should be able to recognise these.

In each case, the posture or gesture is so expressive that the observer should be able to tell from it exactly what the person observed is saying or thinking. In the following pages there are examples of a variety of positions, together with the relevant lines of speech or thought which accompany them.

There is also, moving one step on from Body Language, vital information on Patterns of Social Movement, and a series of easy-to-follow diagrams demonstrate the interplay of people in certain given situations.

POSTURE SIGNALS

"…and I said to him, if that's your attitude, I'm not going to go out with you any more, and he said…"

"As a matter of fact , we did our own conveyancing…"

"Far be it from me to drop into the stereotype of the jealous wife, but…"

"But honestly, darling, I thought we both agreed about the idea of an open marriage…"

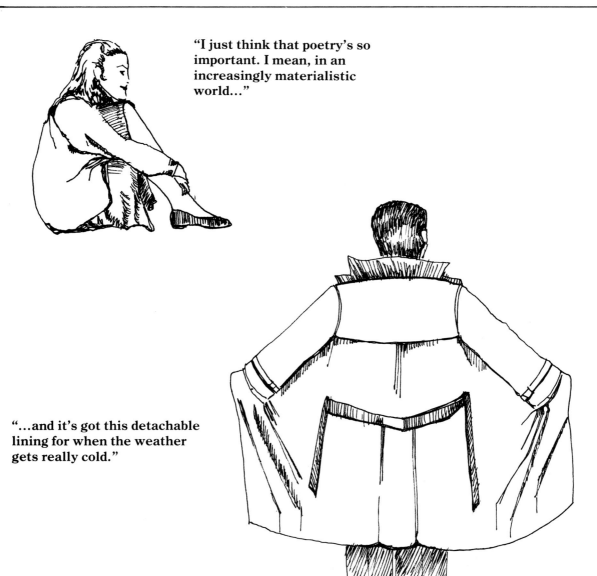

"I just think that poetry's so important. I mean, in an increasingly materialistic world…"

"…and it's got this detachable lining for when the weather gets really cold."

"No, it really does give me a wonderful inner peace, sort of unearthly, and I forget all about the houses and the cars and the au pair and the ponies and..."

"Only another five more years of school-fees to pay..."

HAND SIGNALS

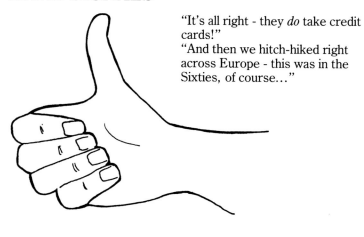

"It's all right - they *do* take credit cards!"
"And then we hitch-hiked right across Europe - this was in the Sixties, of course…"

"It's in the Good Food Guide, of course, and the sauces…"
"And the microchip that does all that is only *this* size."

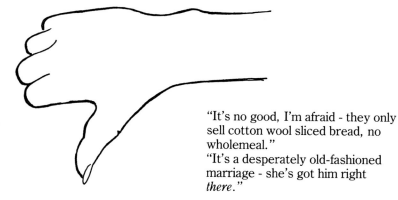

"It's no good, I'm afraid - they only sell cotton wool sliced bread, no wholemeal."
"It's a desperately old-fashioned marriage - she's got him right *there*."

"Of course I'm married."
"The children are doing very well at the comprehensive."

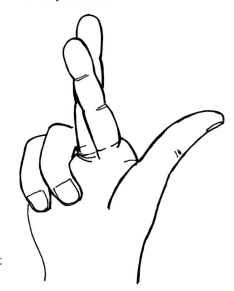

"Give me that doll, young lady. I'm
not having you being moulded into a
sexual stereotype."
"And the palmist said that my
romantic life is really going to take
off in my forties…"

"I think I'm invisible while I'm
driving the car."
"Are you sure this is the right way
to take cocaine?"

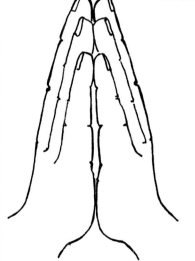

"This is the last time
I use that bloody superglue!"
"The children are doing very well
at the comprehensive."

"And is that one Dolcelatte or Tome
de Savoie…?"
"I'm not having you rotting your
mind with *Dallas*, young man.
Bed!"

FOOT SIGNALS

"Good heavens, the new
neighbours are having a jacuzzi
installed !"

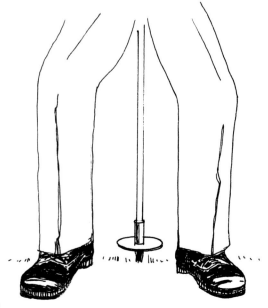

"Come on, Justin, tackle!
Remember, the bigger they are,
the harder they fall…"

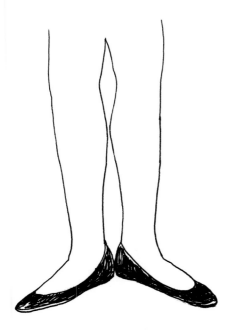

"They predicted a brilliant
future for me, but then I got too tall
and..."

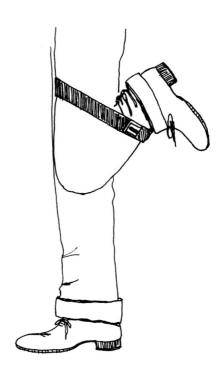

"Look, I know you're the
director, but I still take exception to
your saying that this is over the top
for the crowd scene..."

"…but of course nobody s
going to look twice at a boring fifty-
year-old housewife like me…"

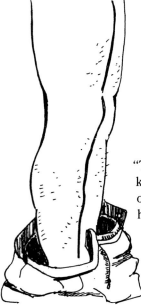

"To be quite frank, doctor, I'd rather
keep it from my wife if I can. You see
on this business trip and you know
how it is…"

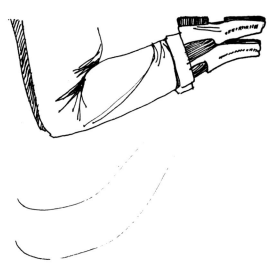

"Samantha's got into Oxford!!!"

"I'm a person first and woman second."

MOVEMENT PATTERNS

PEOPLE-SPOTTERS should be aware of the regular patterns of movement which arise in certain specific social contexts, and will find the following diagrams useful in their study of this phenomenon. In each situation the movement pattern indicated covers a five-minute period. The key describes the people involved in each case.

Hotel Foyer

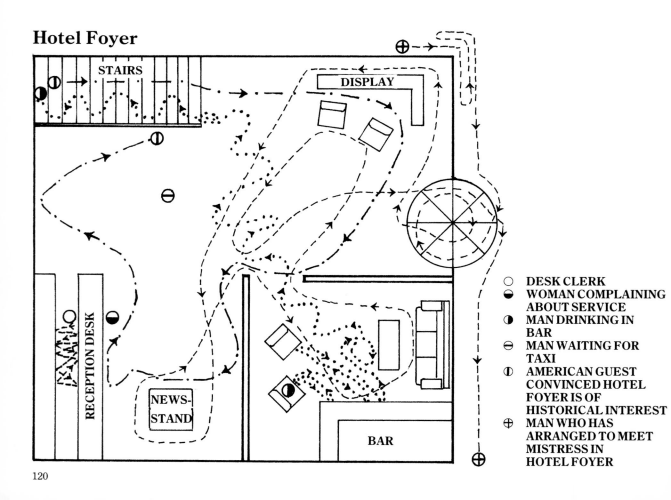

STAIRS

DISPLAY

RECEPTION DESK

NEWS-STAND

BAR

○ DESK CLERK
◐ WOMAN COMPLAINING ABOUT SERVICE
◐ MAN DRINKING IN BAR
⊖ MAN WAITING FOR TAXI
◑ AMERICAN GUEST CONVINCED HOTEL FOYER IS OF HISTORICAL INTEREST
⊕ MAN WHO HAS ARRANGED TO MEET MISTRESS IN HOTEL FOYER

Drinks Party

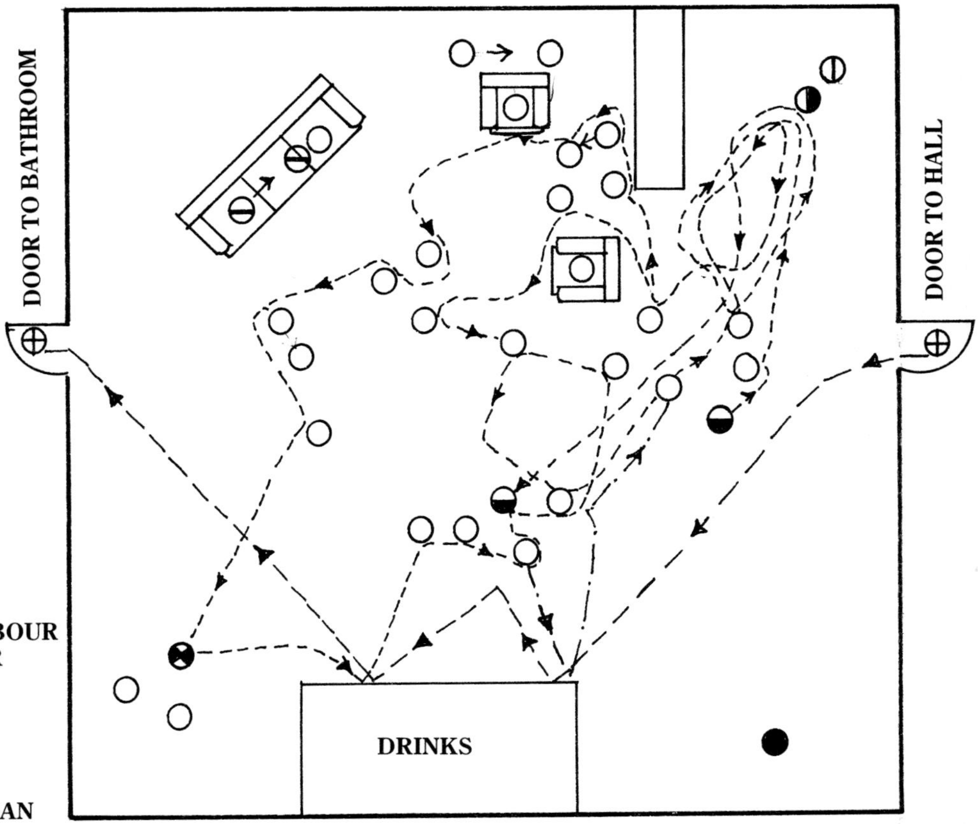

DOOR TO BATHROOM

DOOR TO HALL

DRINKS

○ GUEST
◕ HOSTESS
◑ HOST
⊖ LECHEROUS NEIGHBOUR
◐ PRETTY NEIGHBOUR
⊕ GUEST WHO'S COME
   ON FROM ANOTHER
   PARTY
⊗ MAN TALKING
   ABOUT COMPUTERS
● INSURANCE SALESMAN

Supermarket

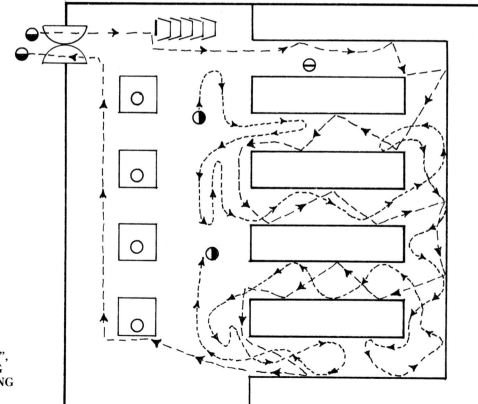

○   **CHECKOUT GIRL**
◒   **EXPERIENCED HOUSEWIFE DOING WEEK'S SHOPPING**
◑   **MAN WHOSE WIFE HAS SENT HIM OUT TO BUY A BAG OF SUGAR**
⊖   ***GUARDIAN* READING", *WHICH* SUBSCRIBING HOUSEWIFE CHECKING INGREDIENTS FOR HARMFUL ADDITIVES**

Tube Train (STUCK BETWEEN STATIONS)

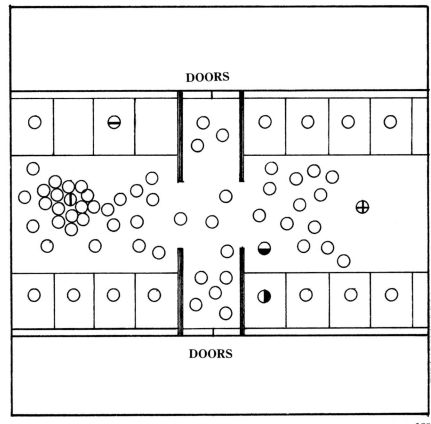

○ COMMUTER
◕ OLD LADY SUFFERING
FROM TERMINAL
FRAILTY
○ HEALTHY YOUNG MAN
⊖ PUNK
⦶ PRETTY GIRL
⊕ MAN WHO HAS
JUST HAD INDIAN
MEAL

APPENDIX I

STATISTICAL GAPS

It is essential that PEOPLE-SPOTTERS should be aware of certain important statistical differences between related Middle Class activities, as detailed in the academic-looking chart below:

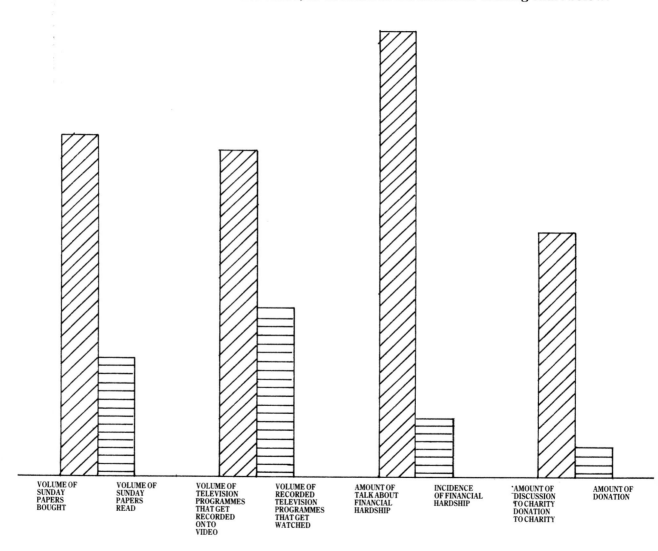

VOLUME OF SUNDAY PAPERS BOUGHT

VOLUME OF SUNDAY PAPERS READ

VOLUME OF TELEVISION PROGRAMMES THAT GET RECORDED ON TO VIDEO

VOLUME OF RECORDED TELEVISION PROGRAMMES THAT GET WATCHED

AMOUNT OF TALK ABOUT FINANCIAL HARDSHIP

INCIDENCE OF FINANCIAL HARDSHIP

'AMOUNT OF DISCUSSION TO CHARITY DONATION TO CHARITY

AMOUNT OF DONATION

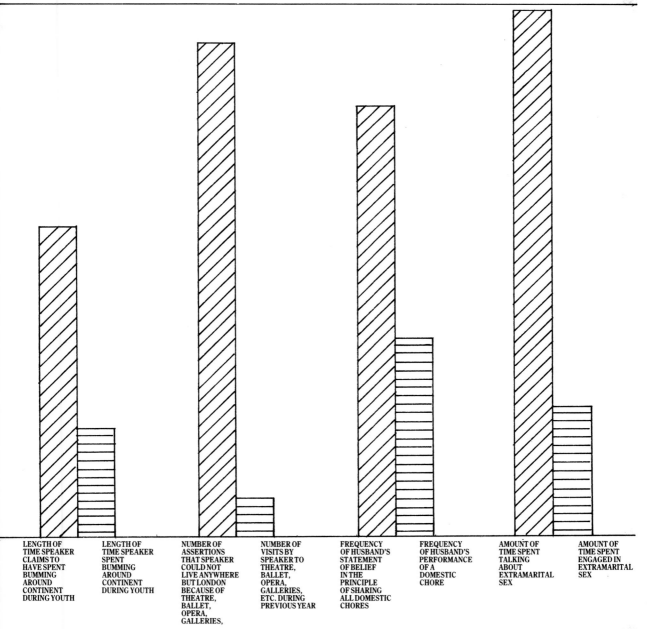

LENGTH OF TIME SPEAKER CLAIMS TO HAVE SPENT BUMMING AROUND CONTINENT DURING YOUTH

LENGTH OF TIME SPEAKER SPENT BUMMING AROUND CONTINENT DURING YOUTH

NUMBER OF ASSERTIONS THAT SPEAKER COULD NOT LIVE ANYWHERE BUT LONDON BECAUSE OF THEATRE, BALLET, OPERA, GALLERIES,

NUMBER OF VISITS BY SPEAKER TO THEATRE, BALLET, OPERA, GALLERIES, ETC. DURING PREVIOUS YEAR

FREQUENCY OF HUSBAND'S STATEMENT OF BELIEF IN THE PRINCIPLE OF SHARING ALL DOMESTIC CHORES

FREQUENCY OF HUSBAND'S PERFORMANCE OF A DOMESTIC CHORE

AMOUNT OF TIME SPENT TALKING ABOUT EXTRAMARITAL SEX

AMOUNT OF TIME SPENT ENGAGED IN EXTRAMARITAL SEX

APPENDIX II

QUESTIONNAIRE

It should be pretty clear to anyone who's got this far in the book how to recognise the PEOPLE-SPOTTER'S quarry, the member of the Middle Class, but for any readers who are still having problems, the following questionnaire will prove a simple and foolproof method of checking on suspected persons. The questions should be asked direct to the suspect, because although the species is notorious for its deviousness, the subjects covered concern such deeply-rooted tenets of Middle Class belief that honest replies will be given instinctively. Instructions on analysing the results are given at the end of the questionnaire.

1. Do you secretly believe yourself to be slightly socially superior to the other people living in your street?

a) No.
b) Well, I suppose perhaps slightly.

2. When you hear that someone who lives in a house has not got a mortgage, do you assume:

a) that they live in a council house, or
b) that they have private money?

3. When someone is described to you as being *"well-educated"*, **do you assume:**

a) that they have had a good education, or
b) that they have been privately educated?

4. If your children are in State education, have you ever been heard to remark that you think it'll be *"a jolly good experience for them in later life"*?

a) No.
b) Yes.

5. When someone is described to you as a *"company director"*, **is your first thought:**

a) that they run their own company, or
b) that they are involved in a criminal court case?

6. Do you regard your doctor as an equal whom you invite to the house socially?

a) No.
b) Yes.

7. Do you regard your butcher as an equal whom you invite to the house socially?

a) Yes.
b) No.

8. Do you introduce a cleaning lady as:

a) a cleaning lady, or
b) someone who helps around the house?

9. Do you watch *Coronation Street* without apologising?

a) Yes.
b) No.

10. Do you watch the *South Bank Show* and then not tell anyone you've watched it?

a) Yes.
b) No.

11. Do you take the price stickers off all food items as soon as they get inside the house?

a) No.
b) Yes.

12. Do you believe that having a sauce bottle on the table is common?

a) No.
b) Yes.

13. Do you believe in the use of milk jugs?

a) No.
b) Yes.

14. Do you believe there is a worse crime in the world than being *"common"*?

a) Yes.
b) No.

NOTES ON MARKING : In each case, the Middle Class person will give the answer b). Anyone questioned who scores more than 50% of b) answers may safely be reckoned to be Middle Class.